A Travel Agent's Guide to

SELLING ADVENTURE TRAVEL

TIPS, TOOLS, TECHNIQUES AND IDEAS FOR BUILDING A PROFITABLE ADVENTURE TRAVEL NICHE

Stephen Crowhurst, CTC

A Travel Agent's Guide to
SELLING ADVENTURE TRAVEL

ISBN-13:978-1724635457
ISBN-10:172463545X

Cover: Stephen Crowhurst
Illustrations by Stephen Crowhurst.

Published by Stephen Crowhurst through CreateSpace

Font: Garamond 12.5

Printed in the United States of America

A Travel Agent's Guide to
SELLING ADVENTURE TRAVEL

TIPS, TOOLS, TECHNIQUES AND IDEAS FOR BUILDING A PROFITABLE ADVENTURE TRAVEL NICHE

Dedication

For Brian Spencer, MBE

It was Brian who introduced me to the great outdoors: camping, hiking, kayaking, canoeing, spelunking and more during my school days at Pollards. It was his love of the outdoors and his enthusiasm for encouraging pupils to get away on weekend adventures that helped me set my sights on travelling the world.

A member of the Keswick Mountain Rescue Team for 45 years, Brian was involved in more than 1,200 rescues. He was also involved in the Duke of Edinburgh Scheme for nearly 50 years. Brian received his MBE at Buckingham Palace for his efforts and contributions.

Thanks, Brian.

TABLE OF CONTENTS	PAGE
Introduction and Welcome	
The Adventure Travel Industry Stats, Facts, Trends	**1**
• Sources of Information	2
• Adventure Travel Trends & Comments	5
Before You Start Planning Your Adventure Travel Niche	**13**
• Know Your Adventure History	14
• Study Books and Maps	20
• Soft, Hard or Extreme? It's Your Choice	21
• Definition of Soft Adventure Travel	22
The Business Adventure Begins	**25**
• Why Would an Adventurer Book with You?	26
• Building Credibility & Your Personal Journey	30
• What Adventures Do You Want to Sell? Choosing Your Adventure Travel Niche	35
• Adventure Activity List	36
• List of Countries	39
• Where in The World Are You Going? Map of The World	42
• Who Is Your Client?	43
• Start-Up Tips	48
Working With Suppliers	51
• Your Suppliers Have Been Doing This Longer Than You	53
Niche Adventures	**57**
• Review of Potential Niche Adventures	58
• Accessible Adventures	60
• The Hiking Adventure	62
• The Independent Adventurer	68
• The Average Adventurer by Generation	69
• The LGBT Adventurer	71
• The Family Adventure	72
• The Solo Adventurer	73
• The Female Adventurer – Women Only	74
• Men Only Adventures	77

• The Hardcore Adventurer	79
• The Extreme Adventurer	80
• The Adventure Group	82
• Religious / Church Groups	86
• Photographic Adventures	87
• Adventurous Art Groups	90
• The Adventurous Cruiser	91
• The Corporate Adventure Group	92
• The Incentive Adventure Group	93
• The Winter Adventure	95
• The Wellness Adventure	96
• The Foodie Adventure	98
• The Birding Adventure	99
• Deep Ancestry (DNA) Adventures	102
• Off Planet Adventures	104
• Glamping	106
Marketing Tips, Tools, and Techniques	**109**
• First Things First – Prep & Plan	110
• Attend Adventure Travel Shows	111
• Foundational Tools	113
• Images and Video Content	114
• Your Website – The Adventure Hub	119
• Get Yourself a Logo	126
• Get Yourself a QR Code	132
• Shoot Those Promotional Selfies	133
• Only Your Best Shots Will Do	135
• Video IS King	136
• Email Marketing	138
• Using Social Media	145
• Movies, Books and Adventure Tourism	150
• Historical Events	151
• Profiling Your Adventure Clients	153
• Newspaper and Magazine Editorial Schedules	159

• Deliver Something Awesome	161
• How Imagery Affects Your Adventure Sales	165
• Choosing Your Camera	172
• Drones and Your Next Adventure	174
• Using Your Adventure Photographs to Sell Even More Travel	175
• Blogging for Adventure Dollars	178
• Press Releases – Your Secret Weapon	181
• Publishing an Adventure Magazine / Travel Fiction	183
• Your Adventure Window Display	187
• Creating Viral Adventure Social Media Buzz	188
• Involve Your Adventure Clients	190
• Images to Screensavers	192
Travel Insurance Coverage for Adventure Travellers	**193**
• Adventure Travel Insurance	195
Things to Do	**200**
Reference Links	**201**
About the Author	**204**
Publications by the Author	**205**

Traveller, there is no path;
paths are made by walking.

Antonio Machado, (1875-1939)
The Quotable Traveler

Introduction and Welcome

You've selected a type of travel that is going places and in one dominant direction, which is UP. It has delivered considerable gains in recent years as you'll read below. Not only that, but there is an adventure for everyone and a niche for you.

The value of the global adventure tourism market is living proof of its growth and its climb in dramatic fashion. Search online for 'adventure travel and tourism studies, reports' and read your heart out. You'll like this bit of news, taken from one of those reports:

The International Finance Corporation estimated the global soft adventure market to be worth $745 billion. The IFC included only hiking, kayaking, rafting, backpacking, viewing nature/ecotourism, bird-watching, diving, and a cultural tourism estimate in its valuation. Another report (not named) went higher. *According to a new report, the global adventure tourism market was valued at $444,850 million in 2016, and is projected to reach $1,335,738 million in 2023.*

The adventure travel market offers you so many niche opportunities to explore, and then, on top of that, there is your passion for a particular destination and preferred adventurous experience. Some adventure selling travel agents are doing very nicely focused purely on packaging what they love to do.

If you are new to selling adventure travel, you should know there are categories describing the severity level of a trip. These levels range from Soft, Hard to Extreme and within those levels, a supplier might also list the grade of difficulty.

Canoeing a meandering river might be classified as a soft adventure. A trek along a steep trail might be listed as hard and getting to the base camp of Everest would be labelled as extreme with fingers crossed.

There's no end to the opportunities waiting for you in the adventure travel market, especially the one that accommodates the niche you prefer. You can sell off the rack, create custom FIT journeys and package your passion, and the passions of your clients. Make it what you want.

Life itself is one great adventure, and you can add to it by studying latest places to walk, hike, kayak, spelunk, climb, fall, ski, river raft and get home in time for supper!

In this book, you will find tips, tools, techniques and ideas for creating both a generic and a niche adventure business. I invented the term niche-within-a-niche which means drilling down through a generic niche/specialty to find a unique and very focused adventure. Current trade terms for my niche-within-a-niche are emerging as: microspecialty, superspecialization and being hyper-focused which generally targets your personal passion. However, there is a certain skill required to search for, find and develop a niche-within-a-niche. Read on.

Take what you can from this book. Make your changes, own it and go sell it! Nothing carved in stone.

Okay, time to follow the arrow. Enjoy.

Steve Crowhurst, CTC
www.sellingtravel.net

Photo credit: Mike Tsirogiannis

Photography and adventure travel go together.
Make sure you include it in all your adventures.

THE
ADVENTURE TRAVEL INDUSTRY
STATS, FACTS, TRENDS
AND MORE

SOURCES OF INFORMATION

It is essential to gather current information — stats and facts as I like to call them — before planning a new department or division and most certainly before starting to sell into a specific niche. All require careful thought, due diligence and data.

Growth is The Good News

The Compound Annual Growth Rate (CAGR) applied to global adventure tourism between now and 2022 is projected to be roughly 45%. Another source puts a projected dollar figure for the worldwide adventure tourism market at $1.3 billion in 2023, registering a CAGR of 17.4 % from 2017 to 2023.

From my point of view, growth is good! The challenge is deciding which part of that growth will affect you as a retail travel agent. The majority of these growth surveys are based on adventure suppliers, destination visitor stats and not so much what travel agents contribute. However — if the suppliers and the adventure destinations are showing, and predicting growth — then that is good for your business and your ideas for creating an adventure travel niche.

research

Gathering Decision Making Information

The following pages review several trends selected from current reports made public by ATTA – Adventure Travel Trade Association, WTO – World Travel Organization, ABTA – Association of British Travel Agents, CLIA – Cruise Line International Association, Kanto Adventures, Intrepid Travel, and Trekksoft Academy.

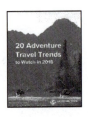

Links to these documents are found at the end of this chapter. Some reports are free to download, others will cost you between USD$99 and four-grand! You see, there IS money to be made in adventure travel. Package some data and sell it for 4G's. Nice.

Sources of Information – Starting with Your Suppliers

[handwritten: Canada / where / re]

The companies who create adventure product for you to sell also have the information you need for planning purposes. Once you identify the companies and products you would like to sell, connect with their sales department and if possible meet face to face to review and discuss the current trends your supplier has identified. Also ask about keywords and slogans your supplier uses and colour schemes that attract would-be adventure clients to the supplier's website then use the same ideas to attract clients to the adventure portal on your own website.

[handwritten: links! / lembah Ind. / NZ Cay / may]

Next – Contact Departments of Tourism

Every department of tourism collects data on who visits their country, where they go and what they do when they get there. Once you decide which country or countries you will be selling, contact the research department and ask for their current trend report. They may ask why you want it. Answer: you will be sending more adventure-based clients to their destination.

[handwritten: who else. Creatia / greece ireland]

Don't Forget Your Existing Clients – The Primary Source *[handwritten: make a list]*

If you have a current client list, then they can offer you primary information and insights into their adventuresome selves. Check with them to survey their adventure travel interests. Gather your research before surveying your client base, then you will know the questions to ask.

Search for Travel Agent Support

When you do your own research and read the reports I have listed, make sure you look for information that supports you as a retail travel agent and the type of adventure travel niche you wish to start. Check with your head office if you are a chain agency or a member of a Host Agency.

Note: Adventure travel associations like ATTA generally work to support the adventure supplier base, destinations and outfitters and not so much the retail travel agent. However, when you visit the ATTA website, you will find that ATTA has partnered with Travel Leaders Network to develop the Active & Adventure Specialist training program. If you associate with Travel Leaders, go to this link for more information.

https://www.adventuretravel.biz/membership/travel-leaders/

Okay, you get the idea. You must dig deep to extract the information you need and want before developing your adventure niche. Now, I have to assume you fit into one of the following profiles:

1. New to selling travel, no past adventure experience, no clients.
2. New to selling travel, some adventure experience, no clients.
3. An existing travel agent with clients – no adventure experience.
4. An existing travel agent with clients, wanting to specialize.
5. Existing adventure selling travel agent wanting to go niche.

There are plenty more combinations, but you're probably sitting somewhere in the above list. So, first things first, let me focus on what you know, and need to know about the current adventure travel segment.

If you are a veteran of the travel trade, you might have the facts and stats at your fingertips. On the other hand, it's always a good idea to top up with current information.

From the reports and surveys I have read, I have gathered the following trends, and to each trend I have added my comments. I have extracted only the trends that have meaning to a small to mid-sized travel agency and ICs. In other words, these are trends a travel agent can develop with low to no-cost marketing.

As you read through this book, you'll find that I cover off most of the trends in one form or another and explain how doable they are. Then in the marketing segment, we'll be exploring, those low to no cost marketing activities that you can afford and not break the bank in doing so.

Far away there in the sunshine are my highest aspirations. I may not reach them, but I can look up and see their beauty, believe in them, and try to follow where they lead.

Louisa May Alcott

ADVENTURE TRAVEL TRENDS AND COMMENTS

The following trends are not listed in order of importance. I've kept it random. Here we go:

TREND: Adventure Tourism Continues to Grow

Tourism, in general, always has, apart from WW1 and WW2, shown growth year after year. Currently, reports indicate that despite terrorist attacks, political upheavals, mass shootings, and natural disasters, tourism has continued to grow.

COMMENT: When you start a travel business, grow an existing one or create a new department, it's nice to know your industry continues to forge ahead. Tourism, travel, vacations and adventure trips are luxuries to some and necessities to others. Even though the industry continues to grow, you must still do your due diligence when it comes to knowing more about your local outbound and inbound selling opportunities.

TREND: Adventure Travel Will Cater to Experiences

According to the Adventure Travel Trade Association (ATTA), the definition of adventure is changing. Risky adrenaline activities are favored 45% less than "experiencing a new culture" in the definition of adventure travel. And travel companies are taking note. Intrepid Travel is seeing a 20% increase in bookings this year for its Real Food Adventure tours which offer cooking classes, wine tastings and local market visits. Day tour company, Urban Adventures, has launched a range of locally-focused shopping ('Made-In') tours for 2018.

COMMENT: According to the report, the definition of the word adventure is changing. So, take note. An adventure, to those that seek it, has always been thrilling, exhilarating and heart pumping. So, you will need to separate in your own mind, how to differentiate between the thrill of a rock climb versus the thrill of meeting a Greek family in Athens for a cooking experience. My adventure would be to climb first, then return to enjoy the foodie experience.

TREND: Solo Travel on the Rise

This year, more adventure travelers will opt to travel on their own. In fact, some reports indicate that one in four Americans will travel solo.

COMMENT: Travelling on your own, going by yourself, now labelled as Solo Travel has always attracted the self-confident man or woman, young, middle-aged or older. The people I have associated with over the years were never groupies. Group tours were for tourists – not adventurers like "us." A few things have changed since then, but not much has changed regarding the solo personality.

The solo traveller still needs you, the travel agent, and especially if you have travelled solo yourself and lived to tell about it!

TREND: Hiking is Number One

The number one adventure in demand is hiking, and this trend pops up more than a few times. Average trip duration, 8 days.

COMMENT: If hiking *is* the number one soft adventure activity then this is excellent news. It allows you to start a hiking niche quite quickly. It also opens up the world to your adventure seeking clients. Hiking is a low impact, easy to do activity that most of your clients can enjoy. There is a hike for everyone: from young to senior to families and friends. Stay in-country or go overseas.

TREND: Custom Itineraries in High Demand

The reported trend is that custom itineraries top the trip types with the highest level of demands. The trip types receiving some interest from clients are "long haul/overseas" trips, along with "environmentally sustainable," "family/multi-generational," and "Solo Traveler" trips.

COMMENT: In the world of retail travel, custom means FIT – Flexible Independent Travel (old term Foreign Independent Travel). That's how we sold travel back in the day and how my buddy Thomas Cook started out in the mid-1800s. Developing and arranging custom trips presents a niche opportunity. It means you build the adventure around what the client wants to do when they want to do it and where. Your niche would become the Adventure FIT Service. Many of your adventure suppliers will work closely with you to arrange a one-off, custom FIT. Some might even allow you to co-brand or white label their products.

TREND: Upwardly Trending Destinations

The list of trending destinations changes depending upon which adventure company is reporting. ATTA has collected data from various suppliers and it shows a growing interest from adventure travelers to visit Eastern Europe, Scandinavia, Southern Africa, and Southeast Asia.

COMMENT: You have to listen to what the suppliers are telling you. They have their finger on the pulse seconds after each beat. They know where the demand is. This information gives you several choices for your FITs. There are close to 200 countries in the world with as many places, cities, locations, wilderness areas, rivers, lakes, waterfalls, mountains, awesome sights and adventurous things that adventurers love to do. You can follow the trends, or in this case, you can go with the destination and activity that fuels your passion.

TREND: Fueling the Local Economy

There is a comment that 66 percent of the per-guest-trip cost is estimated to remain in the local region.

COMMENT: Knowing that when you send an adventure client off on their trip, you are helping to support the local economy, is a good thing. This is a 'feel-good' situation for everyone involved. It is also something you market to your adventure clients and prospects.

TREND: Average Age 49

Regarding adventure traveller demographics. The largest group of adventure travel tour operator clients (41 percent) are between the ages of 50-70. The average age of the adventure traveller reported is 49 years old.

COMMENT: This is information you need. It helps you target would be adventure clients from within your existing customer list. It helps when you are prospecting and marketing outside your client list. It also enables you to select key words and phrases depending upon the generation you are targeting. Someone aged 49 today, is not a Boomer, but a Gen-Xer.

TREND: Majority of Clients use Email or Call

Fifty-one percent of businesses have an online booking system, and the majority of their guests continue to <u>call or email</u> companies directly rather than using online reservation options.

COMMENT: Although this trend is related to adventure suppliers with an online presence, the statement re email and calling in, works for travel agents and suggests that agents like you might need to up their game in terms of email marketing. That is something you will want to review in your marketing plan.

TREND: Being Local is the Ultimate Adventure

As adventure travellers become more experienced, they are increasingly seeking to experience destinations as *temporary locals*.

COMMENT: What was once referred to as immersive and hands-on, is now referred to as *temporary locals*. Current terminology is trendier. More attractive. This is something that solo travellers also like to experience, and the combination of trending ideas is something you can factor into your niche planning.

TREND: Slow Travel

The popularity of "slow travel," when visitors stay for extended periods of time in a destination, will increase, fueled by companies that cater to nomadic workers such as Unsettled and Remote Year.

COMMENT: Well, slow travel used to be just that, traveling the world without a rush. No real time limits. Stopping and staying long term when the place felt like home. Some travellers want to go slow, but they also want it planned – that's where you come in. This trend mentions two companies Unsettled and Remote Year – they are more geared to retreats for Nomadic Workers than what is the true meaning of Slow Travel. It is an interesting concept for sure.

TREND: Adventure Travelers Seek Wellness and Mental Health Benefits in Their Itineraries

Adventure travelers are increasingly seeking experiences that allow them to unplug, focus inward, and tap into the mental health benefits of adventure travel.

COMMENT: This is a trend that appears to be a bit of a challenge – lazing in a spa, for instance, does not ring true as an adventure. That said, there seems to be an opportunity to combine trends once again and probably in this order: a soft to hard adventure outdoor experience followed by a spa or wellness center to relax after the adventure. It's a combination event that could become a separate niche.

TREND: Winter Products

Destinations with winter offerings are seeing substantial increases in arrivals in the colder months— and not just for skiing.

COMMENT: There have always been those clients who like winter anything and as the trend states, destinations such as the Northwest Territories, have created Northern Light (Aurora Borealis) adventures, caribou herd watching and a variety of events – even an ice hotel!

TREND: Increase in Products for Female Adventure Travelers

The year 2018 will see an increased interest in catering to female travelers who seek to bond with other women during their adventures.

COMMENT: This trend is not new but to read of an expected increase is more good news. The female adventure traveller has been outdoors doing her own thing for years. If you are new to selling travel, then you should know that adventures for women have become commonplace thanks to companies like Maupintours, founders of Gutsy Women Travel (GWT) back in 2002.

TREND: Modern Family Dynamics Will Innovate Family Travel

Virgin Holidays launched a new price program for single parents. Intrepid

Travel, which has seen a 16% growth in family bookings, has launched six new family tours in 2018. These tours do not charge more for parents travelling without a spouse/partner. Gone are the days of exclusively two-parent travel offerings – 2018 is the year for all combinations of family.

COMMENT: All good news. Many past adventurers, now married with a family, single with a family and all the various combinations of family, are no doubt driven by the desire to get their kids out the door and into the wild. This too is a great niche to think on.

You can find more trends, both generic and specific and niche targeted when you visit the links below. Chat with your suppliers and departments of tourism and connect with magazines that specialize in your adventure niche. All magazines conduct reader surveys and reports on trends for the adventure or sport they write about.

Here's a smattering of recent survey results published in the trade press by Travel Leaders Group and the Adventure Travel Trade Association.

- 33% of agents said the adventure trips averaged between $3,000 to $5,000 per person.
- 22.5% said adventure clients were spending upwards of $5,000 per person.
- 30% had an average spend of $2,000 to $3,000 per person.
- 66% of respondents indicated trip durations were 7 to 10 days.
- 21% had trip durations of 11 days or longer.
- 86% of respondents grew their adventure travel sales year-over-year in the last three years.
- 50% or more adventure travel customers were aged 41 to 60.
- 60% of the buying decisions were made by women

ATTA defines adventure travel as travel that combines two of three elements: nature, physical activity and cultural exchange. More information can be found here: http://www.travelmarketreport.com/articles/Survey-Shows-Adventure-Travels-Big-Potential-for-Agents

Resource Links:

https://www.adventuretravel.biz/research/2018-adventure-travel-trends-snapshot
www.adventuretravelnews.com/
https://www.intrepidtravel.com/travel-trends-2018/
https://www.globalwellnesssummit.com/2018-global-wellness-trends/
https://cruising.org/docs/default-source/research/clia-2018-state-of-the-industry.pdf?sfvrsn=2
https://www.trekksoft.com/en/blog/9-travel-trends-that-will-drive-the-tourism-industry-in-2018
http://www.travelmarketreport.com/articles/Top-Ten-Destinations-for-Adventure-Travel-in-2018
https://www.technavio.com/
https://www.prnewswire.com/news-releases/global-adventure-tourism-market-expected-to-reach-1335738-million-by-2023-allied-market-research-672335923.html

Adventure travel is trending upwards and the female adventurer is a niche market that's following that trend.

"Wow! Good job we planned in advance. We would never have been able to climb that rock face."

BEFORE YOU START PLANNING YOUR ADVENTURE TRAVEL NICHE

KNOW YOUR ADVENTURE HISTORY

From Lewis and Clark to Daniel Boone, Davy Crockett to George Mallory, John Hunt, to Chris Bonington to Edmund Hillary, Sherpa Tenzing Norgay to Barton Holmes – all of these men opened up routes, pathways, countries and recorded their adventures for us to view today.

You'll notice the above adventurers are all men, but women adventurers were out there, too. From day one, I might add. Take, for instance, Jeanne Baret (1740-1807):

Baret is recognized as the first woman to circumnavigate the globe – but she had to do it disguised as a man. She joined the world expedition of Admiral Louis-Antoine de Bougainville from 1766 to 1769. The French Navy prohibited women on its ships, but that didn't stop Jeanne. She bound her breasts with linen bandages and became Jean Baret. She enlisted as valet and assistant to the expedition's naturalist Philibert Commerçon and travelled on the vessel with 300 men. Expedition accounts differ on when her true gender was discovered. But, by the time she returned to France, Jeanne had seen the world, defied conventions and earned a place in history.

Let's hear it for Jeanne! Way to go, Jeanne! How does that make my female readers feel? Excited? Ready to promote Adventure Travel for Women? Well, hold on. There's more. Visit the links below and scroll down the list of women adventurers, past and current. Everything you read will be information you can use in your marketing and for developing tours based on following in the footsteps of your chosen female adventurer.

https://en.wikipedia.org/wiki/List_of_female_explorers_and_travelers

https://www.besthospitalitydegrees.com/30-most-amazing-women-adventurers-alive-today/

There have been many female explorers lost to history. They did what they did and went where they went with no record left behind. Imagine the women who sailed alone from England to the American colonies back in the 1600s. Makes you shiver a little and even more so when you realize the size of the ship they sailed on. Once you start reading and building your knowledge of who has gone before you, I guarantee that you will better understand your new business from the roots up.

Turning History into Present Day Opportunities

Think about Captain Meriwether Lewis and his close friend, Second Lieutenant William Clark and the expedition that opened up routes to the American Northwest. Imagine that two-year expedition. It wasn't soft adventure that's for sure. If you visit the following website you can read the expedition's timeline which gives you all the stops along the way should you wish to replicate segments as a bespoke adventure tour.

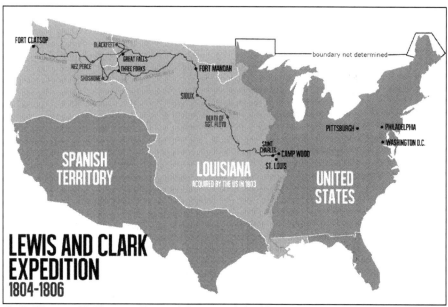

Credit: Victor van Werkhooven - Own work. Image was derived from: Carte Lewis-Clark Expedition-en.png

You will find that so many old reports, journals and books spell out the exact route and itinerary our adventurous forefathers travelled. So easy today to follow in their footsteps on foot, by ten-speed, mountain bike, car, Harley, bus and coach.

If you have history loving adventure hikers amongst your client list, this type of trek would be ideal for them. You would turn this into a custom group FIT and promote it as such. Limited seats of course. The group tour headcount should not exceed twenty otherwise your tour would be bordering on mass-market and lose its appeal.

In the Footsteps of George Mallory and Andrew Irvine

George Mallory and Andrew Irvine climbed Everest. They did not survive. Mallory's body was discovered on the mountain in 1999, seventy-five years after he went missing June 8th, 1924. Irvine's body has yet to be discovered. The thing most everyone is interested in finding is Irvine's camera. The hope is that if the film is salvageable the question of whether or not Mallory and Irvine summited Everest will be put to bed. Here's the cover of a book by Jeffrey Archer, Paths of Glory, a novel based on Mallory's desire to climb Everest. Check on Amazon for a copy.

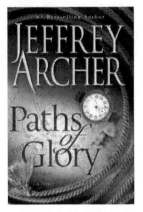

My interest in Everest began as a teenager. Not sure why, but for some reason, I was enthralled by the adventure of the climb. I used to take the train to London and attend talks by climbers such as Chris Bonington of Eiger fame. He climbed the North Face in 1962 and completed an amazing nineteen expeditions to the Himalayas.

Here's a picture of what I was doing in 1962. Climbing Snowdon. I'm hanging out over a 3,000-foot drop to snap my buddy as we prep for crawling across Crib Goch Arete. Not quite a match for the Eiger, but hey, I was out there, doing my own thing and because of those personal accomplishments I could tune into what my adventure clients wanted from their outdoor adventures.

Knowing your adventure roots, studying the history of major milestones in all aspects of adventure travel and documenting your personal adventures is important. No matter how they stack up against the professionals – this personal understanding of what makes someone want to taste adventure travel will become your business foundation. All the better if you can showcase your own adventures to your clients.

Marketing Past Events to Sell Present Day Adventures

Every year there are anniversaries of past events such as the summiting of Mount Everest, May 29, 1953. It's these particular anniversaries that give you something to talk about, blog about and to showcase on your website and in your agency window. Don't forget all social media outlets too.

Here's how you could promote an anniversary event:

**JOIN US ON MAY 29
FOR COFFEE AND A MOVIE
AS WE CELEBRATE THE 1953 SUMMITING
OF EVEREST BY EDMUND HILLARY
AND TENZING NORGAY.**

**GET INSPIRED!
CREATE YOUR OWN ADVENTURE.**

If you wanted to host such a celebration, you could source original film footage (in DVD format) to show in-house. To help you promote your event, search online at Allposters for posters that tie into your adventure niche. Here is a poster for an Everest event.

https://www.allposters.ca/-sp/The-Conquest-of-Everest-1953-posters_i13184272_.htm

An unframed poster sells for $50 or less.

Hosting Your Event in a Movie Theatre

If you happen to be living near a Cineplex, then you could take advantage of their Meetings & Screening services. Still on the topic of showing an Everest movie, you could rent a small theatre for a couple of hours, invite your clients and show the movie. Afterwards, be on stage or up front after the movie to present your new adventure tours and services.

https://www.cineplex.com/CorporateSales/CorporateEvents

Whatever your adventure passion might be, I'm sure there's a movie about it. Source what works for you, then think about using a venue such as a Cineplex or local theatre space at the art gallery or a similar location.

Depending on your age and the type of adventure you are passionate about you may have discovered all you need to know about your personal passion. Now, if you wish to step outside your comfort zone, you could serve the many other types of adventures and the adventurers, in need of your help. Go online and research the long history of exploration.

When you dig deep into the adventure archives, you will find that adventurers travelled on foot, horse and the high seas. They slogged, climbed and hacked their way through whatever obstacle was in their way – or died trying. The sheer determination was incredible. If you are a self-styled adventurer, then you share the mindset of these early explorers.

A New Way to Boost Your Commissions
When you come across old adventure books such as the one shown on the next page, a well-known book about Everest called South Col, check the print date and condition; you might have a winner! My copy on the right is a little tattered – a mint copy shown on the left and signed, is selling for $599.

The adventure market is more than searching for lost tribes. How about searching for lost, old and rare books that are worth a mint?

A traveller's ambition often exceeds his powers of endurance.

Karl Baedeker
Switzerland: The Handbook for Travellers (1899)
The Quotable Traveler

STUDY BOOKS AND MAPS

Your local bookstore will cater to those large coffee table historical adventure books plus you can search online for more. You'll be looking for books ranging from ancient to modern explorers and the routes they travelled. Although most adventure books have been written by men, there are more and more publications featuring women explorers past and present. Women travelling on their own is a niche market we'll explore later.

An adventurer to emulate would be Anthony Dalton. I show one of his books below, (far right) – Adventures With Camera and Pen, a collection of Dalton's past exploits. I include it to nudge you towards publishing your own adventure stories at some point in the future. The sooner you publish and claim the title of author the faster your adventure travel sales will increase. It's amazing what the title of 'author' can do for you and who is attracted to speak to you. Visit www.anthonydalton.net when you can.

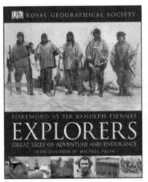  

Old maps are haunting and worthwhile collecting. Imagine arranging an adventure based on a 17th-century map! You get the idea. It's a modern-day adventure with a twist. Build your collection of adventure guides and maps and stories of long-lost explorers who opened the world for you to follow in their footsteps. Remember they gave you something to sell and also gave you an anniversary date to promote. You'll need a year at least to prepare such an event. Start by searching for books and maps related to your personal passion.

SOFT, HARD OR EXTREME? IT'S YOUR CHOICE

No matter what level or category of adventure your clients want, the experience should make their hearts flutter a little. An involuntary gasp of WOW! That's always a good sign. The word WOW is common to adventure travel and it seems we humans are pre-wired to use the word when we are in awe of something.

Hike up or step out of the SUV and go to the edge and peer out and down into the Grand Canyon and 99% of the tour group will say WOW! Some might go overboard and exclaim, "OH, WOW!"

I tell you this because WOW is a terrific marketing word. Not too many WOWs mind you, or you'll sound like a happy dog.

Your clients should be challenged spiritually, physically and culturally. They should return home more enlightened, more in tune with the world, more accepting of others and especially in terms of action, non-action, personal limitations real or perceived.

I remember sending a shy, introverted young girl away on a Contiki tour to Europe and whatever happened during that trip, she returned a new woman. Head up, back straight, slouch gone, eyes alive and looking, searching. This happens to many young people once they are away from home and their social detractors. Being amongst fellow wanderers changes people. Keep this in mind when you write your marketing plan.

I also recall sending a friend's son off to Europe as well. Dad wanted his son to take off and experience travel for himself, then return and get into a career. Well, the son never returned! After the 18-35 tour of Europe, he went to Cyprus to pick fruit for three bucks a day. Then somehow landed a job on a yacht sailing out of the Med' for the South Pacific. Eventually, he went to Australia where he has lived ever since. Dad not happy with his travel agent! But we remained good pals nonetheless.

Hopefully few of your competitors clue into the physiological and personality changes they help happen. Keep this in mind for when you are promoting adventure travel to the younger generations. That low impact trek through a rainforest can change a young person's life.

THE DEFINITION OF SOFT ADVENTURE TRAVEL IS:

"Take me out and thrill me, but bring me home for supper!"

This is your mantra. It will help you focus on selling what most people can actually do and enjoy safely – and be home for supper.

Don't treat this physiological and personality change lightly. Don't let your own adventures become ho-hum. Keep your interest sharp and keen by selling adventure travel to younger people. You can and will help change someone's life and usually for the better. Breaking through the fear of bungee jumping, for instance, can open the door to a whole new personality that had lain dormant.

The situation changes when you engage in selling hard to extreme adventures. Extreme would be bordering on expeditions that could turn out to be one-way. Here are several words and phrases that are generally mixed in with the term, Adventure Travel:

Soft, Hard, Extreme, Green, Eco, Sustainable, Nature-Based, Environmentally Friendly

Primarily you will be selling soft adventure trips. That said, a few clients will want you to book them to the base camp of Everest, or to climb Mount Kilimanjaro (a favourite activity for funding charities). Climbing in the Swiss Alps too would be a hard category, a challenging category for the average soft adventure client.

Let's move on to explore how you can prepare to launch your adventure travel niche business.

Notes:

_____

_____

_____

_____

_____

_____

_____

_____

_____

_____

_____

_____

Hiking is the number one soft adventure activity.

THE
BUSINESS
ADVENTURE
BEGINS

WHY WOULD AN ADVENTURER BOOK WITH YOU?

This is a very important question to answer. Whether or not you've been selling travel for years or just getting into it, there has to be something about you that attracts an adventure client to book with you. What is it? What would attract a group of photographers to you, a family, a solo woman, a gay couple or a corporate Type A who wants to go to the edge?

Let's get back to hiking for a moment. What would attract a group of hikers to contact you first of all, and then book their trip with you or book seats on your Walking Tour of the Cotswolds?

Typically, "we" consumers are attracted by an ad, a slogan, an image, a tone of voice, colour and the look of the salesperson. Once past that initial ooh and ahhh moment, we tend to look at the individual and the company. We click on the About Us tab and check out who we might spend our money with. So now, when the consumer checks you out, what will they find?

They Like You, But Do You Walk the Talk?
Let's assume you're doing well. The prospective, adventuresome client likes you. You look good. Your face (smiling), your eyes (friendly), the way you dress, your voice from the videos played on your website – it all sells you so well. Now, there's one last thing your prospect is wondering: do you actually know what you're doing? They are questioning, whether or not you have visited the places you are selling. They are searching for your adventure travel provenance. They want to see proof of you shooting those rapids or dangling on the end of a rope (in the nicest way possible).

What's Your Adventure Travel Credibility?
If you are new to selling travel but well-travelled with a healthy adventure travel track record then you have a travel history to promote. If that history includes the type of adventure you intend to sell, then this is very positive. Hopefully, you recorded it all in word, video and still images.

If you have not yet experienced adventure travel, then you should know that you will be up against formidable and credible competition. There are adventure travel agents who have climbed, kayaked, walked, hiked, white water rafted and even trekked to the base camp of Everest. Although you have a winning personality, your adventure travel prospects will need proof that you know what you are doing and have hands-on experience. Enter selfies.

Selfies to the Rescue

To enhance your credibility, you'll want to source all those adventure selfies you shot and move them into a special image folder. Those images back up your adventurous claims. From here on, record your adventures in a selfie format, save and file away.

Tip: When you shoot a digital image of you doing something adventurous, and it is a shot that can never be repeated, print it. Yes, you are going from digital to hard copy. This advice comes from professional photographers. You could lose all your photographs if your computer or external drive became corrupted. I now print my best of best images, just in case.

The type of selfie I am referring to is not the one with your tongue hanging out, eyes gone weird and your hands are sporting the devil's horns. Although some clients might like that, you must think strategically here and shoot yourself, not in the foot, but as if you were shooting a corporate portrait. Nice smile, looking into the lens or away. Your best side and angle selected, background helping to sell the story. You are in the shot to prove you were there, but you are not the main star. The mountain peak in the distance is the main star. The thousand-year-old temple gate is the main star. The trail running ahead of you is the main star.

This type and style of selfie can be shot handheld using your smartphone. Job done. Other shots will require a tripod to shoot the right angle and a 10-second delay and/or a Bluetooth remote. Gorilla tripods are an excellent piece of kit, as they wrap around tree branches, posts and perch on uneven ground. There are magnetic versions too for sticking to metal signs for instance. There is even a heavy-duty model to support a DSLR. If you are not a true Selfie Shooter, time to learn how. Also, take time to practice, so you know the best angles to shoot from. You want to show yourself in the best light possible.

Your Adventure Provenance Time Line

When I was frontline and selling adventure travel, I could show my clients that I had been travelling the adventure road since I was a teenager. Yes, back in the days when Ma and Pa would ask, "Where are you going?" The reply would be, "North Wales…" They would answer, "Okay. Be safe. Send us a postcard." And that was it. I'd be off to meet my mates, and we went by a friend's car or train or in Brian Spencer's van. The main thing was, I always shot what was then called a Self Portrait or I had someone else shoot the shot. Other than a selfie, your clients would also like to see the photographs you took along the way.

I can go back as far as my school's outward-bound programs and there's himself, under the arrow – aged 13. Brian Spencer's van in the background.

So, there it is. I could demonstrate that I had been outdoors from a very early age. Now you'll need to dig for your own photos and if you were not the one with a camera, contact the person who was. Ask for copies.

Your mission, if you choose to accept it, is to shoot more selfies with business use in mind, hence the use of a tripod to reduce the fuzzy shots. Practice makes perfect. Things happen so fast, so learn which button to press for those photo bursts. You must score at least one perfect you.

Listing Your Adventure & Travel Accomplishments

You have travelled, you've survived, and you have selfies and other pictures to prove it. Now we need to know where you have been and what you have accomplished. This is important. You can refer to it in your blog postings and also when being interviewed and of course you'll show your client that you have done more than sit on the beach.

Complete this list and add anything else you feel is important:

1. How many countries have you visited?	
2. How many places have you visited?	
3. How many miles flown?	
4. How many cruises cruised?	
5. How many miles hiked?	
6. What was your most thrilling adventure?	

You get the idea. Boast as much as you want as long as you can support your travel history. I cannot stress how important this information is to your marketing campaign and your About Me webpage.

Your Travels Mapped Out

Visuals always work best when selling a client, so document your travels, save as a PDF and JPEG image and then you'll have your content ready to send, post, email and or print and hand out.

If you have an hour to spare, click over to TripAdvisor's Travel Map and create a map you can embed into your website to showcase your travels. To do that, you should be able to click on a code tab, insert the code that TripAdvisor gives you and bingo – your map will appear on your website.

https://www.tripadvisor.com/travelmaphome

Here's a map of my voyages completed by age 19.

BUILDING CREDIBILITY & YOUR PERSONAL JOURNEY

When it comes to selling adventure travel, it pays to have an adventure provenance to showcase to your clients. When you can prove to your clients that you have been out in the wilds, it adds to your overall marketing message.

Where have you been and what have you done that you can boast about in a good way? Remember, those adventure selfies are the best proof that you are the best adventure travel agent in town.

Here's a shot of me at 16 years old on Mount Snowdon, North Wales and I've made good use of this shot over the years to stake my claim such as: "Look, I was out there doing this adventure stuff in my teens!"

If you shot your previous selfies on slides/transparencies or you still have the printed version or just the negatives, be sure to scan them at a high resolution. Make sure you remove the dust before you scan. That small prep work will save you from re-scanning every image.

I'll urge you once again not to be embarrassed when you talk yourself up and showcase your past and current adventures. Some travel agents tell me they do not like to boast, and I get that. However this is all about sales.

Here's one more of me after a thrilling river rafting trip and thanks to the shot taken by Kumsheen I can point out the season/year of the photograph.

Images of your adventures, whether they show you hanging off cliffs, riding a Harley, sitting beside a group of Silverbacks or laughing with Lamas – will inspire others to fulfill their own adventures.

We've beaten selfies to death, so now, other than your selfies, what else can you use? How about stories of narrow escapes or simply stories of wonderment. You will use these stories in your bio, on your About Me webpage and in your blog posts. This content should excite your reader into using your services. When the use of all these tools converge to inform the world about why they should book their next adventure with you, bookings will start to flow.

Your Personal Journey Cred'

It's important that you don't rest on your laurels; keep your adventurous spirit alive. In this way, you can chat with prospects and clients about your next adventure. They need to know you are still running with the pack. So, wherever you are planning to go on your next adventure, this too is something you can talk about, post and promote.

I'm leaving for a 12-day hike across the Scottish Highlands.
***
Get yer boots on and come with me!
Ten seats available.

Can you share your heartfelt desire to travel somewhere to see something, or do something? If you can share, you might attract even more clients by talking about your current personal journey. The above text is all about sharing, inviting and selling ten seats.

Through social media, depending on how well you pitch your next trip, you will gain many readers, listeners and followers. The response is usually a "ME TOO!" response as others decide they want to go with you.

If you write a blog – this type of storyline works great. You do not have to tell all in the first post. You can stretch it out. You can also invite others to tell about their personal hikes across Scotland and let everyone know about your next adventure at the same time.

Be Warned About Starting a Travel Blog

They are easy to start and terribly difficult to maintain, especially if you are planning a daily post. Better to start off posting monthly or bi-weekly and deliver more posts as and when you have the content. If you are not travelling too much just now, you will not have current and exciting content to share. But you could write about various adventures you would like to do. Perhaps you could focus on past explorers or review current adventure travel books and magazines and up coming tour product.

- Blogs are great, and they can tell the world about you and your adventure products.

- Be aware that it takes time to produce a daily or weekly blog and that means you lose marketing time and selling time.

- Blogging during your adventure is probably the best use of a travel blog. Then the content is IRL – In Real Life as the acronym goes. Keeping it in real time and reporting "as it happens" is a great way to engage your adventure clients, build a viral program and referrals.

When you search online for information on how to write a travel blog, make sure you add, *"AND MAKE MONEY."* Too often in the travel industry "we" tend to give things away for free. Yes, still! So, stop that if you're doing it and explore HOW to blog and generate income through sponsorship, advertising and product promotion.

Take a look at these travel blogging sites and
see if they offer you what you need.

http://www.travelblog.org/
http://www.worldnomads.com

Search online for other travel blogging websites.

Words of Advice

If you have not travelled too far afield, my advice is to get out of town and see the world as a travel agent, not as a tourist. When you travel with a travel agent mindset, you would be looking for contacts, the best routes, and eating places in addition to taking in the sights. You do this to gain (and then promote) your first-hand knowledge, take photographs and shoot video for your image bank.

Without that first-hand adventure experience, you will be forever pointing at a brochure page and reading it to your clients versus sitting with your clients and keeping them engaged as you relate what you experienced and what they will experience once they book. The key point here is that you will advise your clients without any props.

There is an argument in the trade that you do not necessarily have to have visited a place to sell it. That is true to an extent. If you can present, sell, overcome objections and close, you can develop a decent adventure niche. However, to have direct experience and be able to articulate that experience is an attraction. It's what causes others to refer their friends to you. Your credibility in the local marketplace is important, and it will set you apart from the other local travel agencies.

Your Adventure Begins

You'll want to know the full list of adventure offerings that consumers have access to, and that includes what your suppliers are promoting locally. Check into the adventures that people actually engage in. Start here with Adventure Finder and review their list.

You'll find what you expect to find, plus a little more such as Adventure Cruises and a variety of soft adventure activities. Print off the list and then highlight the activities that you feel you can sell with passion. You must have that passion exuding from your being. It attracts and it sells.

http://www.adventurefinder.com/adventure-travel/adventure-activities.html

WHAT ADVENTURES DO YOU WANT TO SELL?
CHOOSING YOUR ADVENTURE TRAVEL NICHE

You have a choice of selling any adventure and you can do that by representing all adventure suppliers. At the same time, you can develop a niche – a specific type of adventure that you are known for or want to become known for. That could be a type of adventure (hiking) set in a destination (Japan). With that type of combination, you will set yourself apart from the other adventure travel agents who do not specialize in the same adventure combination you are offering.

The trend reports indicated that hiking was the number one outdoor adventure activity. You could consider hiking to be a safe bet right off the mark – and once again, I'll mention your personal passion, whatever that might be. Before you settle on an adventure niche, it would be worthwhile taking a look at all the options.

The following list presents more than your typical soft adventure activities. So be warned – the list is a collection of activities that people engage in when on vacation, like Naked Bungee Jumping, for instance. The rope burns take some getting used to, but hey! Many of the listings seem similar. Make sure you check them out online. Activities can be combined or developed further into a niche-within-a-niche specialty.

After you have reviewed the Adventure Activity List, think about the countries you would like to promote as your adventure destination(s). In fact, if a particular destination holds your interest you might want to start with that destination, then determine which adventures can be enjoyed there, and be driven by that information. For instance, if you like island life, then select an island and let's go for warmth, so the Caribbean it is. Now, what adventures could you sell to your island paradise? How about scuba? That was easy! It would help if you had a scuba diving provenance. If not, get one. Take lessons. Take selfies. Get certified.

So back to the job at hand. Read through the following list and then move on to make your notes. After that, determine the type of client you wish to attract. Finalize your thoughts on the Planning Page.

ADVENTURE ACTIVITY LIST

Each activity below is either an adventure activity itself or connected to one that could be turned into a niche adventure activity combination. The idea here is for you to review this list and highlight what "speaks" to you as an opportunity. So, carry on – read the list then record your notes in the space provided. Anything new? Different?

ATV/Watercraft Rental
Abseiling/Rap Jumping
Aerobics
African Heritage
Agriculture
Air Safari
All-inclusive Adventures
All-inclusive Packages
Anthropology
Archeology/History
Art/Architecture
Astrology
Astronomy
Auto Racing
Backpacking
Ballooning
Barge/Canal Cruising
Bear Watching
Biblical Tours
Bicycle Touring
Bird Watching
Botany
Bungee Jumping
Butterflies/Lepidopterology
Camel Safaris
Camping
Canoeing/Kayaking
Canyoning
Castles/Palaces
Cattle Cutting, Roping
Cattle Drive
Cave Art
Caving
Christian Tours

Christmas Tours
Church Tours
Clans
Collectors Tours
Conservation
Country Inn/Guest Ranch
Covered Wagons
Crafts Tours
Cruise/Shore Excursions
Cruises, Expeditions
Cultural Expeditions
Desert Expeditions
Dhow Sailing
Disabled
Dogsledding
Dolphin Research/Swim
Driver-guide
Duck Hunting
Dude Ranch / Farm Stay
Ecology
Ecotourism
Elephant Ride
Environmental Education
Equestrian Tours
Extreme Sports/Stunts
FIT's
Family Groups/Tours
Farmhouse
Festival Tours
Fishing / Fly Fishing
Flightseeing
Fly-in Charter
Fly-in Hiking/Rafting
Fly/Drive Package

Foliage Tours
Four-Wheel Drive
Fox/Stag Hunting
Garden Tours
Gem Collecting
Genealogy
Geology
Ghost Town
Glacier Tours
Goat Packing
Gold Panning
Gorilla Viewing
Gourmet/Gastronomy
Grandparent/child Tours
Hang Gliding/Soaring
Health & Fitness
Heli-Rafting
Heli-Ski
Heli-Trekking
Helicopter Tours
Hiking
Historic Houses
History Tours
Holistic Health
Honeymoon Adventures
Horse Breeding
Horse Carriage Tours
Horse Racing
Horse Riding/Packing/Trek
Horticulture
House Boating
Hovercrafting
Hunting
Ice Climbing
Iceberg Viewing
Ice Fishing
Island Resort/Vacation
Jeep Safari
Jet Boat Expeditions
Jet Skiing
Jungle Expeditions
Jungle Lodge
Kon-Tiki Rafting

Language Study
Lewis & Clark Trail
Lighthouse Tours
Literary Tours
Llama Packing
Marine Biology
Martial Arts
Medicine
Metaphysical
Military History
Mine Tours
Motorcoach Tours
Motorcycle Rental
Motorcycle Rental/Touring
Motorhome Tours
Mountain Bicycle Tours
Mountaineering
Multisport
Music/Dance
Mystery Tours
Myth & Folklore
National Parks
Native Americans
Natural History
Nature Reserve
Nature Trips
Northern Lights Viewing
Oenology/Wine Study
Oktoberfest
Outdoor Skills/Adventure Training
Overlanding
Painting
Paleontology
Paragliding
Penguin Viewing
Photographic Tours
Pilgrimage/Mythology
Pioneer Skills
Polar Bear Watching
Polar Expeditions
Railway Trips
Rainforest
Ranching

Reindeer Safari
Religion/Spirituality
Research Expeditions
River Cruises/Expeditions
River Lore
River Rafting
Rock Climbing
Rodeo
Round the World
Running/Jogging
Safari/Game Viewing
Sailing Schools
Sailing
Scuba/Snorkeling
Sea Kayaking
Self-drive Tours
Seminars
Shamanism
Shipwrecks
Single Travelers
Ski Clinics
Skiing /X Country
Skiing/Downhill
Skydive
Snowboarding
Snowmobiling
Snowshoeing
Solar Eclipse Tours
Solar/Alternative Energy
Spa/Hot Springs
Space Travel
Spiritual Tours
Sports Camps
Sports Tours
Surfing
Swimming

Tea Tours
Teachers' Tours
Textile Arts
Trekking
Truffle hunting
Ultra-Light Flying
Vegetarian Tours
Veterans
Videography Tours
Villa/Chateau Rental
Vintage Airplanes
Vintage Cars
Volcano Tours
Walking Tours
Waterskiing
Weekend Escapes
Whale Watching
White Water
Wild Horse Watching
Wilderness Courses
Wilderness Lodge
Wilderness Vacations
Wildflower Viewing
Windjamming
Windsurfing
Winery Tours/Wine Tasting
Women's Tours
World Cup
World Series
Writing Workshops
Yacht Charter, Bareboat
Yacht Charter, Crewed
Yoga/Meditation
Zoology
Zorbing

WHAT ARE YOUR TOP THREE ADVENTURES?

1. _Scuba_
2.
3.

LIST OF COUNTRIES

Afghanistan
Albania
Algeria
Andorra
Angola
Antigua and Barbuda
Argentina
Armenia
Australia
Austria
Azerbaijan
Bahamas
Bahrain
Bangladesh
Barbados
Belarus
Belgium
Belize
Benin
Bhutan
Bolivia
Bosnia and Herzegovina
Botswana
Brazil
Brunei
Bulgaria
Burkina Faso
Burundi
Cabo Verde
Cambodia
Cameroon
Canada
Central African Republic
Chad
Chile
China
Colombia
Comoros
Democratic Republic of the Congo
Republic of the Congo
Costa Rica

Cote d'Ivoire
Croatia
Cuba
Cyprus
Czech Republic
Denmark
Djibouti
Dominica
Dominican Republic
Ecuador
Egypt
El Salvador
Equatorial Guinea
Eritrea
Estonia
Eswatini (formerly Swaziland)
Ethiopia
Fiji
Finland
France
Gabon
Gambia
Georgia
Germany
Ghana
Greece
Grenada
Guatemala
Guinea
Guinea-Bissau
Guyana
Haiti
Honduras
Hungary
Iceland
India
Indonesia
Iran
Iraq
Ireland
Israel

Italy
Jamaica
Japan
Jordan
Kazakhstan
Kenya
Kiribati
Kosovo
Kuwait
Kyrgyzstan
Laos
Latvia
Lebanon
Lesotho
Liberia
Libya
Liechtenstein
Lithuania
Luxembourg
Macedonia
Madagascar
Malawi
Malaysia
Maldives
Mali
Malta
Marshall Islands
Mauritania
Mauritius
Mexico
Micronesia
Moldova
Monaco
Mongolia
Montenegro
Morocco
Mozambique
Myanmar (formerly Burma)
Namibia
Nauru
Nepal
Netherlands
New Zealand

Nicaragua
Niger
Nigeria
North Korea
Norway
Oman
Pakistan
Palau
Palestine
Panama
Papua New Guinea
Paraguay
Peru
Philippines
Poland
Portugal
Qatar
Romania
Russia
Rwanda
Saint Kitts and Nevis
Saint Lucia
Saint Vincent and the Grenadines
Samoa
San Marino
Sao Tome and Principe
Saudi Arabia
Senegal
Serbia
Seychelles
Sierra Leone
Singapore
Slovakia
Slovenia
Solomon Islands
Somalia
South Africa
South Korea
South Sudan
Spain
Sri Lanka
Sudan
Suriname

Swaziland (renamed to Eswatini)
Sweden
Switzerland
Syria
Taiwan
Tajikistan
Tanzania
Thailand
Timor-Leste
Togo
Tonga
Trinidad and Tobago
Tunisia
Turkey
Turkmenistan

Tuvalu
Uganda
Ukraine
United Arab Emirates
United Kingdom
United States of America (USA)
Uruguay
Uzbekistan
Vanuatu
Vatican City (Holy See)
Venezuela
Vietnam
Yemen
Zambia
Zimbabwe

WHICH COUNTRIES SUIT YOUR ADVENTURE IDEAS?

THE POWER OF THREE

Have you thought about having three locations, three destinations where your chosen adventure products can be enjoyed? Remember you must always have a backup, or two, should your main destination be compromised in any way.

WHERE IN THE WORLD ARE YOU GOING?

Shade in the countries you have designated as your adventure destinations. Start thinking about transportation routes and how you can combine different adventures to the same destinations.

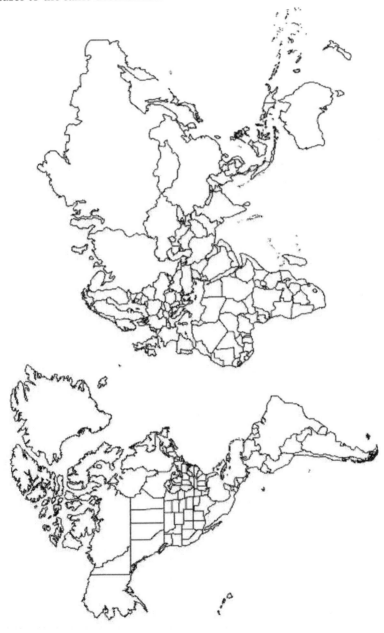

WHO IS YOUR CLIENT?

Profiling the customer you want to attract is always an interesting activity to go through. To target a specific customer profile, you must first decide on the adventure itself, followed by the location and pricing. You cannot determine the client/customer profile without first understanding what it is you intend to sell. Once you have a blueprint of the type of client to attract, you can research how best to market to them.

1. Decide on your adventure product and destination, pricing etc.
2. Profile the people who currently enjoy this adventure.
3. Study what makes this profile purchase adventure travel.
4. Plan a marketing strategy to attract this customer.

The process is to think about each person/generation that has the means and the time to buy the type of travel you intend to offer at the price point or price range you have selected. Consider where they live and how you will communicate with them based on how they prefer to communicate with businesses like yours. How do they want to receive their news? Ask them directly once you have identified them.

For the moment do not get caught up, or ahead of yourself thinking about how to take your adventure travel offers worldwide. Concentrate on selling locally – it's easier and cheaper to do so. If, however you live in an area where few people live, then you'll expand your marketing to the next city, state, province or territory. Keep in mind the old business adage that your business is 'within a 5-mile radius' – it is within this 5-mile radius of your office that most of your adventure clients will reside.

Once you build an awesome website and online marketing campaign, you will, by luck, chance and design, attract adventurers from across the country – and eventually from around the globe. In the meantime, your business will be literally outside your agency door or your home-based office.

You can access adventure traveller profiles by contacting your suppliers and also adventure magazines who conduct timely readership surveys. If you are specializing in kayaking, contact kayaking magazines. Make a note as to who are you going to contact?

Which profiles are you interested in? Check off all that might contribute to your decision.

- ☐ Baby Boomers
- ☐ Gen-X
- ☐ Gen-Y
- ☐ Gen-Z
- ☐ Families
- ☐ Singles
- ☐ Gay
- ☐ Straight
- ☐ Religion Biased
- ☐ Race Biased
- ☐ Activity Biased
- ☐ Age Biased
- ☐ Sex Biased
- ☐ Affordability
- ☐ Trip Duration
- ☐ Has friends
- ☐ Has connections
- ☐ Can refer
- ☐ Easy to deal with
- ☐ Will pay fees
- ☐ Live close by
- ☐ Language Biased
- ☐ Other
- ☐ Other

You could check them all – but then trying to attract that many profiles would drive you nuts! However, you could, if you wished, take on all comers and market to everyone. Think it through. If you intend to specialize, there will be a certain profile that best fits your business idea.

Let's go with the following profile as a place to start:

Gen-X – Woman only – All lifestyles
All Races – All Religions

This profile is obviously focused on the female adventurer. The agent of record is probably female and Gen-X herself. She might feel she can best communicate with women of her own age/generation and she is accepting of all races, lifestyles, religions and so on. If she wanted to widen the scope of the profile she could add all ages.

When you go through this exercise, you will not find it easy. Again, you could be all-inclusive, and that will take you only so far. When you come to writing your blog post or creating an ad slogan, how many ways are you going to write it to reach everyone who could book on your hike around Japan, for instance?

Drilling down to what makes sense to you, based on your personality, age, generation, knowledge, experiences and plans for the niche adventure is something you must consider doing. I'm assuming that you are a one-person show with limited funds.

If you are running a fully staffed retail agency selling adventure travel with a staff of ten, then for sure you can take on all profiles, and no doubt have the money to fund separate ad styles to capture the eyes, hearts and minds of all adventuresome customers and prospects.

Note: The word 'biased' in the grid refers to your business bias and the type of specialized tours you would like to sell. For instance, if your ideas where Religious Biased, then your tour groups should attract people of the Catholic faith. Sure, a Buddhist could join, but mostly the trip itinerary would celebrate the Catholic faith. I'm reminded of the tours around Kyushu Island of Japan and the story of the Hidden or Secret Christians as depicted in the movie Silence. Walking and hiking in that area is a whole new adventure that has not yet been promoted. For sure 'everyone' might like to go. However, the true essence of the place and what happened historically would resonate with those of the Catholic faith or religious history buffs who wanted to see where the actual events took place.

The Generational Grid

Six generations make up our current society. Each of those generations harbour would-be adventure clients. Here are the birth years for each generation and their current ages (A: eldest, B: youngest) as of 2018. The Years Left column represents the number of years left to travel out of 80, the average longevity for North Americans. Women tend to live five to eight to ten years longer than men.

GENERATION	BORN BETWEEN		A	B	TRAVEL YEARS LEFT	
SILENT	1922	1945	96	73	(16)	7
BOOMERS	1946	1954	72	64	8	16
GEN-JONES	1955	1964	65	54	17	26
GEN-X	1965	1976	53	42	27	38
MILLENIALS	1977	1995	41	23	39	57
GEN-Z, iGEN	1996	2018	-	22	-	58

Notes: As each generation ages, the older people fill the gaps left by the passing generation of seniors. Currently, that would mean Baby Boomer seniors will be replaced by Generation X seniors. Health starts to deteriorate later in life decreasing the ability to travel. Client succession planning is important. Remember, you will also be ageing!

PLANNING PAGE

At this stage, you have made some decisions as to what you will sell, to where and to whom. Jot down your thoughts and ideas below, and then we will move on to how you can work with your adventure suppliers. After that, we will take a hard look at various tours and marketing.

Type of Adventure/s	
Destination/s	
Customer Profile	
Other	
Other	

Is There a Doctor in the Tent and Where's the Loo?

Better factor these two questions into your planning. It's what most travellers say are their top two priorities. This is very important.

About the Doctor: If it's possible, offer a discounted rate to attract a doctor to travel along with the adventure group. He or she is part of the group in every respect and only when someone falls ill will you request their professional assistance. You should, if heading overseas, subscribe to the doctors-on-call programs and also have SOS apps installed on your phone. The latest IOS for iPhone will send coordinates to an emergency response center. Your Travel Insurance Provider should also offer a Doctors-on-Call program. Check the IAMAT program too. They offer English speaking doctors worldwide. https://www.iamat.org/medical-directory

Regarding the Location of Toilets: Out in the wilds, the next tree might do. Some countries have installed toilets along the hiking routes. When entering a town, or city, its best to ask the locals or check online for an app like this one: https://greatbritishpublictoiletmap.rca.ac.uk/

Many establishments, cafes, pubs, etc., around the world, now lock their toilets. You have to ask for a key. Having a toilet map is essential. Learning how to use one of those pop-up loos is a must if you will be informing your clients how they work. So sooner rather than later, give one a try. If no luck, back into the forest you go.

For Women Only

In the wilds or in public toilets, women can be at a disadvantage when going to the loo. This device/gadget is worth mentioning to your female adventurers. Let each person decide for themselves if it's of any value. It's called Go-Girl – a urination device for women. It allows a woman to pee standing up which offers an element of safety and escape if needed.

https://go-girl.com/

START-UP TIPS

The adventure travel business would appear to be one tourism segment that is destined to grow and keep on growing. When you follow the links to review current research, stats and facts you will also read about trending destinations that are expected to grow their adventure tourism. One of those destinations might be the right one for you.

Now, when planning a new business or adding to an existing one, you should know, if you have not done this before, things change. So, despite all the potential, you must, repeat *must*, have a Plan B. You must expect the unexpected and know what to do when **splat** happens.

Expecting the Unexpected

What can I say about this well-known quote? Few people are prepared for the unexpected? Sure, there are road signs and escape routes to higher ground should a tsunami ever turn in your direction, but what about in business? How do you prepare for the unexpected? The answer lies in researching the country and destinations you plan to sell.

Before you commit to arranging your product offerings to any destination on your list, make sure you have studied the stability of the government, if civil war could break out, the local people's view of tourists, any religious conflicts, weather patterns, earthquake potential and of course the safety factors for women and gay adventurers travelling in a group or solo.

When you book your clients through an existing adventure supplier, you can more or less rely on the fact that the supplier has done their due diligence and confirmed their chosen destinations are safe. That said, who can prepare for an 'out of the blue' terror attack? That type of incident aside, your supplier's destination choices should be trustworthy.

This type of preparation removes the stress of the unknown. You should also participate in the adventures you intend to sell and travel the itinerary and routes before you sell them. You should NEVER send one person or a group off on an adventure you have never experienced first-hand. Even if you sell a supplier's product, experience it first. It will cost you in time and money however, you will reduce the chances of litigation.

You will also increase your chances of selling more adventures when you have been there, done that and can articulate from experience to your clients what they can expect. This knowledge falls under the heading of credibility and this is part of your overall adventure travel provenance.

Now, some suppliers will accommodate you and include you on an agent or media FAM. In other cases, you may have to pay your way at a discounted rate. As this is your new business niche, you should build a fund to invest in your education and hands-on experience.

I know some agents balk at paying for their FAMs but once again I state this is not a vacation. This is a cost of doing business. I can also state that your self-financed, first-hand experience and knowledge gained will, as mentioned above, reduce litigation and increase sales.

Notes:

Here's one of my favourite "get out there" quotes.

Life's a pretty precious and wonderful thing. You can't sit down and let it lap around you... you have to plunge into it; you have to dive through it! And you can't save it, you can't store it up; you can't horde it in a vault. You've got to taste it; you've got to use it. The more you use, the more you have... that's the miracle of it.

Kyle Samuel Crichton

WORKING WITH SUPPLIERS

YOUR SUPPLIERS HAVE BEEN DOING THIS
A LOT LONGER THAN YOU HAVE

Depending on your business plan and what you believe to be the best adventure format for your exciting niche, I'd suggest you research which adventure suppliers offer what you would like to sell and then arrange a meeting. Chances are they will not come to you. You'll need to prove yourself before that can happen. Unless, perhaps a BDM is in your neck of the woods and senses you have something to offer them – like sales.

You could communicate by phone and dial direct, however in my book it is always best to visit your prospective suppliers in their office. This accomplishes a couple of things. It shows you are interested and willing to invest in yourself and you understand the importance of making connections. Whereas many new start-ups try to fool very knowledgeable travel trade veterans with the old song & dance that goes something like, *"I'm the best thing that's gonna happen to you! I'll bring you groups! I can really sell!"* They've heard it all before. They've seen it all before. End of conversation. So that approach just ain't gonna work.

Meet with Their Group Department

Most suppliers have realized the value of operating a group sales department dedicated to servicing travel agents. Make the call, arrange an appointment and go visit. That's right. You go to them. You'll do this for several reasons: you should meet the group department as the agents working there will help you over time. You should also meet the head-office team and if it is possible, meet with the marketing department.

Spending a day or two at a supplier's head-office is worth every cent. You should return with names and contact information, ideas for marketing, knowledge of what sells best and when, and hopefully customer profile data so you can target similar profiles in your area. Learn everything you can about the keywords, slogans, phrasing, colour schemes and layouts they use to promote the products you will be selling.

Be sure to ask for training in the supplier's adventure travel insurance offered in their brochures. You must accommodate your adventure client with insurance and you will decide between coverage from your regular insurance provider or the coverage offered by the supplier. You have to be sure your client's activities are covered 100%. Remember: slips, trips and falls are the main causes of accidents and death in the adventure business. Car accidents remain the main "killer" of tourists worldwide.

Meet your BDM

Your Business Development Manager or supplier sales representative is your link to everything your supplier offers. Befriend this person and tap into their knowledge and skills. Request planning data when it is available. Also ask for advanced warnings for when new adventure products are being released. This will give you time to prepare your marketing, and hopefully launch a timely campaign soon after the supplier makes their announcement.

When it's time to create your marketing plan and list the activities you will engage in to attract bookings you should be well ahead of the game. Plus, when you run into a challenge, as you will, you can always call your contacts that you met personally at HQ.

What's the Best-Selling Adventure and Why?

If you have not yet decided on a niche activity, ask your new-found supplier friends which tour or activity is selling well this year, and why. Go with a successful trending adventure to start your adventure travel selling career. You can branch out later on and create your own product using the packaging services of your suppliers.

Supplier Comparisons

As you review which suppliers to sell, you'll want to create a comparison chart so that you can check off what each supplier offers. You'll want to make sure that they offer your type of adventure, to your preferred destination. Additionally, you should question their accident insurance coverage, the pricing and what is NOT included.

Another topic to explore is the certification levels of the guides escorting your clients into the woods or across the desert.

Trip leaders and wilderness guides should all have advanced wilderness first aid and CPR certification. They should all carry top-of-the-line satellite phones and regularly participate in on-going training to keep their survival skills sharp.

Attend All Training and Conferences

This may cost you, or there may be funding to finance your attendance. If you belong to a host group or belong to a chain agency, then chances are you will travel on company dollars. However you get to attend, attend. Stay the course and attend every session. Learn as much as you can. Your commitment will be noted by your suppliers.

Free Trips to Taste the Adventure

Usually, you will be required to prove you have sold the supplier's product. At some point in time, with sales under your belt, you may get that magic email that invites you on an all-expense paid adventure.

If you ask for free trips without having sold anything you'll be considered an amateur and not taken seriously. As mentioned previously, pay your own way to start and ask if a travel agent's discount could be applied.

Marketing Data

The supplier will release a certain set of numbers to you that are for the most part generic but will help you better understand when to launch an ad campaign. Based on their information you could start promoting. Using the supplier's peak and valley data you would promote on the high side, before and at the peak and not when the bookings are in decline as the season tails off.

Arranging Your Own Groups on Spec

Speculative groups are not for the new agent on the block. Even some travel veterans find this hard to do. Going on spec means you will buy seats in advance, hold them under deposit and attempt to sell them before the seats are recalled and placed back into inventory.

Speculative groups are a tough road to haul. It is not for the nervous type. You'll need to be very sure of your selling and closing capabilities. Once you build your niche and have a proven track record in generic adventure groups then you should have all the expertise you need to go spec.

Ways to Work with Your Suppliers

Your suppliers can serve you in many different roles and present you with a list of services they can provide. Some suppliers will offer nothing more than product and brochures. They are focused on their own business plan.

What you are looking for in a supplier is this:

- ☑ To draw on their head office experience in arranging niche groups.
- ☑ To block X# of seats on a scheduled tour and sell it as co-branded.
- ☑ To add a custom sightseeing activity just for your clients.
- ☑ Have the opportunity to rebrand the supplier's product as your own.
- ☑ To access co-op marketing dollars.
- ☑ To have a BDM attend your adventure events.
- ☑ To have the supplier's reservations team sell into your tour.

When you visit your preferred adventure supplier, you can ask these questions. It's important to show you have done this before, or, that this is your first time, you are learning the group travel trade and would appreciate the supplier's help.

No doubt you are well connected with the adventure suppliers who call on you or reach out to you from wherever they are based. There are local suppliers, and then there are global suppliers who operate out of an office in most of the world's major cities.

When you find the companies that interest you, you know the drill. Email right away and ask about their products, check them out online, watch their videos, check social media for complaints and finally, the money. Ask about commission rates, group rates and FAMs.

National Geographic Adventures

If you would like to sell NG Adventures, photography tours etc., you can, and they pay 8% - 10% depending on the tour product. I had this confirmed by NG. Go direct for more information.

http://www.nationalgeographicexpeditions.com/about/contact

NICHE ADVENTURES

REVIEW OF POTENTIAL NICHE ADVENTURES

In this section, we'll explore the various and most common types of niche markets and also take a look at extreme and different adventures you might consider selling. The majority of what you will sell however will fall under the category of soft adventure. The definition of soft adventure is your guide. It is important to bring your adventure clients home for supper because you need them alive to buy more adventures from you.

The definition of soft adventure travel represents the category of adventure most of your clients will want to book. The slogan, "take me out and thrill me but bring me home for supper" has been around for a very long time, and yet it remains tongue in cheek within the trade. It does, however, speak the truth.

Your clients do want to be thrilled, and they do want to return home safely. The soft adventure products you choose to sell should be tried and tested and boasting an excellent safety record.

Climbing Mount Everest presents a possibility of not returning for supper. That is not soft adventure. You would need to scale down to something similar to what I'm doing in the above photo – pyramid gazing at Giza. Hey, now that could be a new adventure! Tour title: Giza Gazing.

As and when you design your agency's adventures, then, like your suppliers, you too must make sure you can bring your clients home safely for supper.

We know most adventures have inherent risks whether they are soft or extreme. When the adventure is extreme, the worst and the unexpected are expected. Unexpected events related to soft adventure can creep up on you or your client and be devastating. For instance, a casual day hike through a forest could end on slippery rocks – a disaster waiting to happen for the uninitiated.

The rate of devastating possibilities increases when rocks are wet, when rapids run at Grade 6 and rain causes mudslides. Slips and trips, bears on the trail, a sudden tidal surge, falling off a chair and even misunderstanding a cultural expectation that leads to a brawl. All of these things can happen, and they do, but rarely. The point is, as an adventure selling travel agent, you must be aware of what can happen and plan around them. You will need the answers to all things safety-related and be well aware of the types of travel insurance coverage available to your adventure-going clients.

I went looking for other adventure travel definitions and asked my well-travelled friend, Steve Gillick, founder of Gillick's World and Talking Travel and publisher of TalkingTravel e-Magazine, for his thoughts. Here are Steve's comments:

• Adventure Travel consists of the experience of interacting with the people, the culture, the history and the land, and coming away with an appreciation, understanding, empathy and determination to think of the world as a community where people are people and a smile is the language we all share.

• The interactive component in adventure travel may be one activity, as simple as a stroll, a walk or a hike, or it may consist of a series of activities that vary from the casual to the challenging.

• Ultimately, adventure travel represents a more in-depth experience for the traveller and one that will stay with them for the rest of their life.

Source: Steve Gillick, TalkingTravel.ca

ACCESSIBLE ADVENTURES

Sometimes we miss the obvious. When you are fit, healthy and able-bodied you can be seduced into looking at life from just your point of view. You may not realize there are others who are not as able-bodied as yourself, (and if fate knocks on your door, you might join them at any time), yet they also desire to travel and experience a challenging adventure.

It was some years ago when I attended a conference and met disabled travel agents. One of those agents, a young woman, was very successful in the group segment. The previous year, she had sold, closed and sent off 300 groups.

Another agent was a young man in his thirties. A businessman, suit and tie, and maneuvering his wheelchair with skill. When we chatted, he told me "I was just like you, Steve, well, before the car accident..." and that was when fate knocked on his door. His life changed. His career and his business took a different turn as he developed a niche to handle accessible traveller's needs.

There are generic travel agencies who will book accessible cruises, hotel stays and tours when requested. It is more of a sideline. Then there are agencies, travel agents and tour companies who specialize not only in accessible travel but in accessible adventures. If you have a mind to go for it, this could be a very rewarding niche for you.

Types of Accessible Adventures
The Accessible Adventurer can ski, sit-ski, hunt, fish, scuba, hike, kayak, canoe, swim, zip-wire, sky-dive, ride pack-horse, hand-glide, skipper a motorboat and canal barge. The more you look into the types of adventures the accessible adventurer signs on for, the more you'll feel like expanding the offers.

There are adventure programs that bring together both physically disabled and non-disabled adventurers who, working together, climb, hike and more. In many cases using a special wheelchair called the "Joëlette."

Accessible Suppliers
Over the years it has always been that someone managing from a

wheelchair ran an accessible travel company. In other words, very few travel agents understood the accessible travel business accept those who had become disabled in some way.

Another travel agent I met at the conference was sight impaired or as she said, blind. Yet there she was telling me all about the groups she sends off around the world to enjoy the world through their remaining senses: sound, smell, taste. That caused me to research such tours, and sure enough, there were places of wonder such as gardens where a person could guide themselves using tactile assistance like stones, walls, wooden posts. Their sense of smell worked overtime, as fragrant flowers wafted their scent to entice them closer. It is amazing how the accessible traveller copes and the number of adventures that await them.

Here's a link that will take you to a listing of companies
that serve the accessible adventurer:
http://www.executiveclasstravelers.com/1/adventure_travel.htm

Right, over to you. Keep searching and researching to discover whether or not this is a niche you could take on. Also explore the certification offered here:
http://www.specialneedsatsea.com/agents/sng-cata-certification/

Here is a work of passion. This book is amazing in its content. More for the person travelling, however worth reading from a travel agent's point of view. Click to the link below then look for this text: **Download** Lonely Planet's Accessible Travel Guide (First Edition) in PDF format (2.8 MB) - the download link it right there for you to click.
http://www.accessibletourism.org/?i=enat.en.news.1910#commentArea

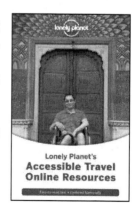

Lonely Planet's
**Accessible Travel
Online Resources**

THE HIKING ADVENTURE

Hiking we are told is the #1 stand-alone adventure that also leads to other adventures and other destinations as your adventure clients decide to do more. The hiking activity is popular in almost all countries from Japan to the UK to America to Bosnia to Canada. I've hiked in those same countries and as diverse as they are, making friends along the trail is commonplace.

Another plus in developing a hiking niche is the cost. Your clients can get into hiking at a reasonably low financial outlay. A pair of hiking boots or walking shoes, rain gear, a backpack and a few more essentials and your clients are ready to go when they receive your email.

When planning your hiking niche beware of how your suppliers grade their trips. The grading of hikes ranges in difficulty so you must be aware of the differences and the level of fitness required to enjoy each hike. Here's how **Kanto Adventures of Japan** grade their hikes and fitness levels and thanks to David Niehoff for giving me permission to reprint.

Level 1	Level 2	Level 3
Walking with a low chance of injury. For this level, sports shoes are okay.	Mountain climbing with the possibility of occasional use of the hands or chains or ropes to move up the route. Little potential danger is encountered. Hiking Boots recommended.	Scrambling with increased exposure. Handholds are necessary. Chains, ladders, and other aids may be in place on the route to navigate safely. Exposure is present, and falls could result in serious injury or death.

Kanto Adventures also grades the fitness levels for their hikes:

The fitness level is very important for you to know and mention to your clients. You do not wish to be facing a legal situation whereby a client could not participate in a hike due to lack of fitness. Your suppliers should advise you on this topic and also supply a client sign-off form to confirm they are fit enough to go on the hike they have chosen. The grading of hikes is not something you do. The responsibility for grading each hike or adventure falls on the shoulders of the supplier. Your responsibility is in knowing the grading and forewarning your clients.

A: Easiest – Suitable for people of all ages who are in fair condition. Elevation gain of less than 300 meters and less than 10km of distance total.

B: Easy – Suitable for people of most ages who have a basic fitness level. Elevation gain of less than 600 meters and less than 12km of distance total.

C: Moderate – Reasonably fit hikers who get out at least once a month should be able to do this level. This level would be considered easy for frequent hikers. Elevation gain of 500~1,200 meters and a maximum distance of 15km in a day.

D: Challenging – Regular hiking experience is required to participate in hikes at this level. Elevation gain of more than 1,000 meters and potentially more than 15km distance in one day. Combination of significant elevation gain and long distance make this level a challenge for many.

E: Very Difficult – Long distances and big elevation gains make this level. High fitness level is required because speed will be important to complete

Visit Kanto Adventures here when you can:
http://www.kantoadventures.com/
Make them your #1 adventure supplier in Japan.

Walking the UK
Your hiking clients would enjoy my old walking haunts and one of the best companies in the UK for this is English Lakeland Ramblers.

http://ramblers.com/

The Lake District is one of my favourite places to walk, hike, ramble...call it as you see it. This area of the UK is a wonderful place to hike and your hiking clientele will love you for the suggestion.

Options

Companies like English Lakeland Ramblers offer your clients various options such as guided, self-guided and customized. Knowing this you can market each option accordingly. The customized version would be an FIT, arranged to suit your client's time frame, energy level and hiking habits.

Be sure to look for these types of options with any supplier you choose to do business with.

Here's a link to many more walking/hiking suppliers.
Some just about sneak onto the list with one short walk.
Others are actually in the business of walking-hiking tours of various durations, grades and destinations.

https://www.stridetravel.com/hiking-walking-tour-companies

Sitting at the edge of the frozen Beaufort Sea.

Hiking / Walking Clubs

Guaranteed there are hiking and walking clubs close to where you live and work and sell travel. Could be a local hiking group who are interested in hiking further afield. There could be a hardier few amongst the many who are looking to upgrade their current level of adventure.

If you are a hiker yourself, then why not start an agency hiking club? Not in competition to the local clubs, but as a marketing tool to attract local hikers. You might need to add a specialty of some kind, so think about your own interests. I always mention photography as that's one of my personal passions. Photography and hiking go together so nicely – except for the weight of all the gear, and that leads "us" to a specialty. Here it is:

Hiking iPhoneography Tours

The latest smartphones have wonderful built-in cameras, and that's all you need to capture the sites when hiking the trails. You could also promote smaller point and shoot cameras too, but the smartphone is the attraction. You might include training in iPhoneography as you hike and trek the trails. It's a unique combination to think about.

Grading Your Hikes

Just like Kanto Adventures of Japan, it would be a good idea to grade the hikes you promote. In this way, you can pitch the various levels in your marketing to local hiking club members.

Is There a Doctor Close By?

Don't forget the doc! He or she is a selling point. Most tourists today, even the adventurous ones, want access to quality medical help as and when and if they happen to fall, slip, trip or get bitten or suffer an allergy outburst.

Put an ad in the local press to attract a local doctor and keep them listed for when a tour is ready to set off. Arrange a discount for them and let them enjoy the hike like everyone else. You may never need their services however it's a nice touch to add to the overall offer.

Here's a poster layout idea you could copy.

OUR ADVENTURES ALWAYS INCLUDE A
DOCTOR

We know that most adventures have an element of danger that includes slips, trips and falls, insect bites, allergic reactions to plants and more – that's why we always have a doctor travelling with us a regular member of the adventure group. We also know where the clean toilets are! Yes, the number one 'must have' listed by thousands of travellers.

Call us today to book your next adventure.

WALK & TALK ADVENTURES

If you are a local doctor, contact us and join our next adventure.

Best Hikes, Walks and Trails

One thing is for sure; you will never run out of places to hike. As I explored online, searching for the best hikes, I was inundated with links to the best 25, the ultimate 50 and on it went. Here's a couple of links for you to explore and after that go online and do your due diligence. Search through all the hiking trail websites to look for the niche that excites you.

https://localadventurer.com/25-best-hikes-in-the-world-bucket-list/

https://www.wanderlust.co.uk/content/the-worlds-best-walking-routes/

From Hike to State of Mind

Some hikes, trails and pathways listed are more than a one-day outing. Many are seven days, and some are up to thirty days.

When you scour the internet for the trails you would like to follow, often you will come across one or two words that leap out and say, "Use me, I'm a slogan!" Like this: *The Camino isn't a walk, it's a state of mind. Some see it as a spiritual undertaking, others as a physical test; for some it's all about the camaraderie at the albergues (pilgrim hostels).*

It isn't a walk, it's a state of mind.

That slogan is great. Use it for marketing any of the hiking products you intend to sell. The walk has to be something special and more than likely have a philosophical or religious component to it.

NOTE: Always check if the words or slogan have been trademarked or if a copyright icon is beside it. If so, then you cannot use them. But, you could create a similar phrase/slogan.

THE INDEPENDENT ADVENTURER

An independent adventurer would be a client who knows what they want, where they want to go and when. They have done it before and they can do it again, which begs the question: are Independent Adventurers worthwhile chasing? Do they make good clients?

If this prospective customer does know what he or she is doing, has done it before, then chances are they will book direct. If they do need any specialized information from you, you'll charge them accordingly. They might need help in getting a permit, or special hotel/accommodation that's not with Airbnb or listed with the IYHA and cannot be booked via an app. And they may want to pre-book and add something ordinary to their trip. The self-guided adventure product is ideal for this client.

Courting the Independent Adventurer is a good thing and here's why:

- They can and will top up your knowledge of the adventures they enjoy, plus they can advise you on and about the destinations they visit.

- Their knowledge is your next sale. Truly. You can turn around and advise your not-so-independent adventurers, *"Hey, great news, this was just told to me by someone who has been there and walked that trail…"*

Another reason to stay in touch with your Independent Adventurers is this – they age! Yes, like everyone else, there comes a time when they do not want to do it all themselves. They also want to chase after new experiences and join an adventure/hiking group for the comradery. What else? Well, yes, they might even write and excite your current client base into getting out into an adventure of their own. They could speak at your next presentation, and post to your blog, too.

You could start by arranging a local event. Have suppliers attend, invite your Independent Adventurers to speak, then you take the podium and WOW your audience into joining your next tour or arranging an adventure FIT.

THE AVERAGE ADVENTURER BY GENERATION

I don't usually subscribe to anything 'average,' but here we'll use the word to broad brush across all generations who are out there on the trails.

Based on your research you will know that the current crop of surveys, reports and studies tend to box in each generation and itemize what makes one adventurous person from each generation, different from the others.

The focus seems to be on Gen-Y / Millennials as DIY adventurers, and that's okay. When you are young and have the tech as close as your phone, why wouldn't you arrange your own adventures? But then, as Gen-Y age, as did Gen-X and the Boomers before them, the DIY changes to YDIFM, or, You Do It For Me. That's right. Things change. Lifestyles change. A few Gen-Y'ers will carry on with DIY while the rest will want a little more pampering. It happens to every generation.

I have to say that from my experience, no matter the generation or where a person sits age-wise, there are basic instincts that rise to the surface when faced with a glorious sunrise, sunset, a churning sea, miles of sandy beach, or tall ancient trees. In a word, it comes out as: WOW!

Put all the present-day techno gadgets and apps to one side and get to the basics of being outdoors and it is that WOW experience that thrills 99% of adventure clients. And that is all you need to keep in mind when you market to any generation. Sell the WOW!

You could, if you felt compelled, add a note to your specific targeted audience such as Gen-Y to make sure Wi-Fi is available at the hotel, hostel, inn or wherever they are staying. Then again, there is a rising desire to be free of, and away from, anything that doesn't communicate without the use of lips.

A hands-free adventure might just hit the marketing sweet spot. A no-phones adventure. Just like the old days when those hardy adventurers, who broke the trails and scaled the mountains, stayed in touch by shouting.

The No Tech Adventure
Can you imagine anyone leaving home without their smartphone? Not

really, and that phone can prove to be a lifesaver. However, you could go as far as "allowing" your clients to carry their phones with them, BUT when it comes to certain aspects of the adventure, such as asking for directions, ordering meals, learning a few words of the local language then the deal is, the rules are, you have to try it "old style." Use those lips and voice-box and ask, talk, say, request and smile. Discreet selfies are allowed.

Off the Grid 100%

There are clients demanding to be 100% away from anything tech. No phones thank you very much. They want to be at peace with the surrounding landscape and not have the silence penetrated by yapping fellow adventurers calling home to say what a great time they are having. This no tech, un-plugged adventure could be a niche market.

How to Use Your Smartphone on the Trail

So now a quick reversal. There is also a niche in showing newbie (and veteran) adventurers how to use their smartphone in the wild. There are tools/apps in that phone that anyone heading outdoors for the first time should know how to use:

- Maps
- Flashlight
- GPS
- Morse Code
- Location Finder
- Emergency apps

Apple included an emergency call app in iOS11. It can be set up through the Health app and also by pressing (for my iPhone7+) the on/off button on the right, five times. Using some of these apps will rip into the battery life – so, a charged battery booster (or two) is a must-have piece of additional kit to carry.

Marketing to each generation does require a tweak here and there. It will pay to read the reports that explain the differences. You can start here and click to the link below.

https://www.adventuretravelnews.com/marketing-and-selling-adventure-travel-to-millennials

THE LGBT ADVENTURER

Welcome to a niche market that has been 'there' for as long as anyone of any other lifestyle has been out in the wilds. Alyson Adventures was a company I came across back in the late 1990's and has since merged with HE Travel. The gay adventurer has been out exploring, hiking, climbing and adventuring for decades and it has been only recently that straight agencies have realized the potential of this market.

Gay or straight, perhaps this could be a brand new niche for you. If you happen to be gay yourself and have not yet made a move into adventure travel then give it some thought. Your clients may be booking their adventure trips elsewhere or direct with suppliers. If you think there is an opportunity to attract this niche clientele to your agency then survey your LGBT client list to determine the overall level of interest.

Can a Straight Agency Sell Gay Adventure Trips?

The response is: can a gay travel agent sell to a straight client. Answer: YES! Of course. It doesn't matter what your lifestyle is, or race, creed and religion. If you have the knowledge and the personality to treat everyone with respect, you've got business. So, if you are a straight travel agent/agency then you might have a brand new LBGT Adventure Niche waiting for you.

Contact your preferred suppliers and ask about their gay adventure groups and also their individual tours. If your preferred suppliers do not offer such a product, search online and deal directly with the suppliers, such as HE Travel, who create adventure tours for gay clients. When it comes to marketing, check the words, slogans and images other gay travel companies are using. Then get OUT and sell!

https://hetravel.com.
https://www.iglta.org/outdoor-adventures/
Worth reading: http://www.alysonadventures.com/about.htm

The LGBT acronym has grown to include more identities that need to be understood and respected. LGBTTIQQ2S includes: Lesbian, Gay, Bisexual, Transsexual, Transgendered, Intersexual, Queer, Questioning, 2-Spirited. http://lgbtq2stoolkit.learningcommunity.ca/

THE FAMILY ADVENTURE

A new term: lone-parent family. In Canada, lone-parent families make up 19.2% of Canadian households with children. The United Kingdom's Office for National Statistics states there are around two-million lone-parent families in the UK. In the United States, a current report tells us there are thirteen-million single-parent families living there.

The travel industry is quickly catching up with adventure offerings listed as lone, single and solo-parent adventures. Hotels and resorts have come up with their solo-parent pricing and specialty activities. The lone mum or dad will be able to enjoy adult conversation with other lone parents while their child/children are enjoying mixing with other kids.

The Family Adventure could be a niche for you if you're inclined to know and understand what divorce means to a family unit, the pressure and the challenge of vacationing alone with 'the kids.' It ain't fun. There's a learning curve involved. As a Solo Family Adventure Travel Agent, you could be just the answer to a newly divorced parent who needs a break.

Start the Club
Why not? Promote locally that you are starting a Solo-Parent Travel Club and host an evening at a local hotel. Nothing grand other than coffee and cookies. Be frank and honest and present your ideas to your audience and then ask for input. Once you know how your ideas sit with your audience, you can survey their travel needs and dreams and then arrange for more events with suppliers who service single parent travel, to present their products.

Consent Forms
Don't forget; the travelling parent must have a documented agreement from the ex' allowing the travelling parent to travel with their child. Check out the travel consent form at the link below.

https://www.us-passport-service-guide.com/minor-travel-consent-form.html
https://www.intrepidtravel.com/ca/theme/family/single-parent

Check out Family Travel Association: https://familytravel.org/

THE SOLO ADVENTURER

It's the only way to go for the self-confident. More often than not, when small groups set off, they split up based on personality clashes and when reasons for travelling differ. Much of this is unknown until the group is on the road. Some travellers set off as a groupie then become a solo traveller. One of the predicted trends is for Solo Travel to grow to an 'all-time high' and apparently, according to Google, the terms 'solo travel' and 'travel alone' have had the highest search rates recently.

The surge in going it alone has not gone unnoticed by suppliers. It seems the solo traveller/adventurer might just be coming into their own. Finally! The days of paying surcharges and single supplements could be gone. A cruise line out of the UK is installing solo cabins in a new build to launch in 2019. https://travel.saga.co.uk/cruises/ocean/find-your-cruise/solo-travel.aspx

The Solo Niche
Not all solo travellers/adventurers are DIY'ers. Many to most still require assistance in arranging their trip. That's where you come in of course, and hopefully, you are up-to-date with the suppliers who are now catering to single/solo travel.

Name your niche, come up with your slogan. What will it be?

Single Travel // By Yourself Travel // JustYoo
Costs are SOLO you can't afford not to go!

The Solo Adventurer will fit any profile, age, race, creed, religion and lifestyle, so once again, there could be a niche-within-the-niche waiting for you to kick it into gear. I'll set the scene here with Solo Women Adventures for African American Women who love Photography. Okay, that's my input. You can create other profiles, themes, destinations and activities. Come on. You can do it!

Solo Traveler World
This website is a 'must' to visit: https://solotravelerworld.com/

THE FEMALE ADVENTURER – WOMEN ONLY

Women-only vacations have been available for many years now thanks to those intrepid women who couldn't wait for the travel trade to catch up and did their own thing. Over the years I've seen fly-fishing trips for women only, trekking, hiking, kayaking, climbing and every other outdoor activity you can think of and guess what – those adventures are still selling and filling up.

Start with Education / Training

Let's say you fancy the fly-fishing niche, or ramping it up a little, you decide on mountaineering. Whatever you choose as your niche, you might just have to educate your newbie adventure female clients into the fold. For that, you can arrange a training camp. That's right – there are fly-fishing schools: https://www.montanawomensflyfishingschool.com. The same applies to mountaineering and kayaking and other activities.

Search for it online and bingo! Now you can put together your first training camp, and from there you will expand to the real thing such as kayaking local rivers and work up to kayaking the greatest white-water rivers in the world. Paddle local – white-water international.

The Corporate Woman

Female achievers like to go to the edge for the better view. Offer an adventure that leaves the office grind behind to tackle a local mountain or an overseas trek. If it's mountains you're after, you have enough in North America to last you ten years or more. Then there are the overseas trips to be amongst mountain vistas worth climbing. Try the European Alps or go large and head for Nepal. The Female Corporate Adventurer is a niche.

Previous Reports

Women travelling together are travelling with their friends and that's a very important note to remember when marketing and especially when using a social media channel to promote your tours.

This niche shouts referrals, small groups and tying into the mass media promotional events such as Women's Day and Mother's Day.

MOTHER'S DAY ADVENTURES

HAWAII BOOKING NOW!
CALL US AT:
WOMEN WANNA SURF
1-800-WOM-ENR2

https://wildwomenexpeditions.com/
http://www.travelandleisure.com/trip-ideas/adventure-travel/travel-companies-for-women
https://www.rei.com/adventures/trips/womens-trips

Mother and Daughter Adventures

Here's a niche within the Women Only niche. You can carve out an adventure tour for mothers and daughters and send them off on an independent tour, or book them on a ready-made adventure group departure. Search for them under Women Only Adventures such as those fly-fishing packages, or trekking in the UK, Japan or Europe for instance?

Use graphics with a touch of humour to get your message across. Humour always adds to the promotion and helps boost response.

MEN ONLY ADVENTURES

Standby for some wild and whacky ways to adventure. As you may have experienced along your own personal trails, when men get together, all hell can break loose, especially when those sixty-year olds are thinking like sixteen-year olds. Yup. When men book an adventure trip, make sure you sell that travel insurance coverage!

From hiking basic trails to heli-skiing, to white-water rafting on Nepal's Sun Kosi river, you can promote any macho-styled adventures and there will be a line up when you set the challenge. That's right. You have to sell the "Are you up for it?" and the "Are you fit enough?" challenge. It's that male psyche that you are challenging, and now I'll just add: *be careful what you ask for – you may get it.*

Despite all the bravado that tends to go with men-only adventures you must still bring them home safe and sound for supper. There are always those tour members who will go closer to that grizzly for a selfie!

The Cerebral Male Adventurer
On the other hand, you may decide to deal only with the male adventurer who thinks before doing anything dangerous. These would be men who will not endanger the lives of their fellow adventurers or go against local customs and culture, especially when it comes to treating local women with respect. The thinking adventurer prefers to engage every sense they have, reserving their voice for later. When you are out in the wilds enjoying the view, you don't need someone piping up, breaking into the tranquillity to talk politics or about the office.

Who You Get Depends on the Tour Title and Slogan
If you sell a 'thinking man's' tour, you'll more than likely fill up with the type of adventure client you expected. Try to qualify your slogan with a tagline.

Cultural Adventures for Your Senses
See, Touch, Smell, Taste & Listen

(Speech is left out for a reason – if you talk too much you're not listening. Chances are you are disturbing the natural space for others.)

Father and Son Adventures

Just like the Mother and Daughter niche-within-a-niche, there is a niche for Father and Son adventures. These too can be a fishing trip along a local river or up to Alaska or British Columbia, Canada to fish for those huge salmon.

The concept for these types of adventures is usually to help father and son bond, communicate, explore together and to get a better understanding of each other beyond home, work and the ever-present smartphone.

For the male bonding type of adventure, factor in a certified counsellor/adventure guide on the team. That way when the dad and son don't see eye-to-eye, they have access to the proper support.

An adventure such as rock climbing is an activity that will show both the son and the father how to help and support each other if that is an underlying challenge. Or, the father and son could be outdoors, on that rock face enjoying their time together as intended.

Pull me up son. That's the way!

THE HARDCORE ADVENTURER

Here's where you, meaning retail travel adventure agents, split from the activities this adventurer wants to do. Now keep in mind that at some time in their lives, even hardcore adventurers slow down and seek a not so hardcore thrill.

Hardcore adventurers are just behind extreme adventurers. There's a good chance a hardcore adventure is a one-way ticket. That's right. Death is riding on their shoulders. One slip, and it's a severe injury to all-out death. The type of adventure these brave souls seek is offered through companies who are prepared for the ultimate challenges. Check this NG list out: https://www.nationalgeographic.com/adventure/lists/9-worlds-most-extreme-adventures/

Swimming with anything that can go "chomp" or "double chomp" would be a hardcore adventure. Heli-skiing would rate up there too. Storm chasing for sure. Wingsuit gliding and base jumping are two more activities to test how hard your hardcore really is.

They Know Each Other
It would be more than difficult to break into any of these select hardcore activities unless you participate yourself – then you could pitch your agency as a possible agency of record. But, you never know. There might be one or two people in your neck of the woods who seek this level of adventure and would like you to arrange it all.

Capturing a hardcore adventurer to spend their $20,000 bucks with you is like trying to secure a world cruise client with $100,000 to spend. They are out there, BUT why would they spend that money with you? What would attract them to you? You have to have something extra going for you. You are either in their financial five and know who they know, or as mentioned above, you participate in the hardcore event and become recommended.

Other than that, there's little chance of securing such an adventure booking. Be patient, wait until they go soft, then swoop in and sell those soft adventure tours.

THE EXTREME ADVENTURER

Just like their hardcore buddies, this group of adventurers run with the same pack. They will know each other, they will deal with the leader of the expedition, and their adventure will have a support group, a base camp of sorts and a cameraman or three to record the event for post-adventure commercial sales. That type of arrangement is not generally within the scope or remit of what a typical adventure travel agency can manage.

But, (yes there is always a but), you can use this event to showcase what an extreme adventure is. Use the event media to send chills and thrills up the spines of your soft adventure audience. It's like watching a Warren Miller ski film. You'll be on the edge of your seat and tired out at the end of the film. Knackered by seated adrenaline! The very next day though, you are looking for that Warren Miller level of adventure. And that's how you can tap into the extreme adventures and expeditions posted to YouTube and recorded on DVD for retail sales.

How to Use Extreme Adventures to Market Soft Adventure
Next, if you would truly like to rub shoulders with these extreme adventurers and you can afford their fees, invite them to speak at your next conference, group gathering or arrange a flight and take your adventure clients to see the speaker wherever they are telling their story. Could be Las Vegas, could be a travelling event that comes to your city.

When these extreme adventurers write books, publish photographs and videos of their adventures then these too can serve as excellent marketing tools. Although you and or your adventure clients may never go the extreme route, you can enjoy the accomplishments of others and as a group even donate to the expedition. That too can be used in your marketing to help grow your soft adventure customer base. How do I know this? Because I've done it. Check out the image on the next page.

The postcard opposite was sent to me by Jamie Clarke who, along with Alan Hobson, climbed Everest. We had Jamie and Alan speak at a Uniglobe conference and present the story of their expedition, how they handled the challenges and the outcomes. I haven't met up with Jamie or Alan since that conference, but you know what, I've never forgotten the experience.

After the conference, the agency owners in attendance were keen to be more adventurous in their businesses; the agents eager to sell more adventure products. See if you can attract someone who has been there, done it, can prove it and tell it. Their passion will spill over to your audience, who will have itchy feet to get themselves outdoors. Booked with you of course!

THE ADVENTURE GROUP

Group travel is a profitable segment of the travel trade, and it's an exciting one too. On the flip side, it can also kill your business – which is not the best strategy to follow. You have to do it right if you intend to profit. Adventure travel is not for every client, however, amongst those five-hundred names on your client list, there must be 25 to 50 who seek something different, exciting and challenging.

Promote Your Group Adventure Services First
There's a couple of ways to enter the adventure group business, and the safest way is to advertise and promote the fact that you can arrange a group departure for an adventure-loving group. In other words, an existing group, such as a group of photographers who want to go north to photograph polar bears, caribou or just the tundra. They catch your ads, and they call.

Not much could go wrong with that call as long as you can satisfy their needs, and you know your way around Alaska, the Yukon, Northwest Territories and Nunavut. It also pays to have contacts in the North such as http://www.touchthearctictours.com/ owned and operated by Susan Mercredi, President.

The Speculative Route
Going on spec' as we say, is not for the faint-hearted. It means putting your money where your mouth is and laying out a couple of thousand dollars to secure several tour seats and airline seats with the hope that you can sell out your tour. Going on spec' is a killer of travel agencies unless you have someone to guide you from start to finish. If the tour does not sell out, you'll be left hanging in more ways than one.

Travel the Safe Route to Start
That's right, just like climbing a rock face. Go safely to start. When your skills and experience allow it, you can try the speculative route. The safest route then is to create your group adventure services and promote them. Like fishing, you'll use the right bait to catch and land a ready-made adventure group. You'll use your social media skills and your graphic design talents, too. Here's something you might have created using Web Graphics Creator. It's a program I use often. It gives you just what you

need to whip up a quick promotional image by selecting a background or several layers, add or change the text that comes with the design and then you can drag and drop various elements into your promo to give it some oomph. Visit: www.webgraphicscreator.com

Promoting Your Credibility

You'll remember my comments about your adventure provenance and keeping a photographic record of your outdoor activities. Well, here's where you can put them to good use. It's time to do a little boasting and promote the fact that you were 'there' that you climbed this and hiked that and go back in time when you were a kid, to last week's adventure.

Humour tends to work well too. Not overly so and no expletives which seem to be entering social media just a tad too much. Keep it clean, and you will win the business.

If you use Photoshop Elements (the poor man's version of Photoshop) and understand how to use layers, then you can construct a promo piece that will sell your services, give the reader a chuckle and for sure, if done right, your artwork will go viral and hopefully point a few more adventure seekers in your direction.

Be sure to read online about using Photoshop Elements. Being able to use tools such as PSE is mandatory for present-day travel marketing.

Fake Views!

Yes, that's me, looking as if I'm perched on that iconic stone slab which was about 3" in length, and layered over a cloud shot. Don't forget – you must explain the FX'd shot somewhere in your accompanying text.

WHEN IT COMES TO PHOTOGRAPHIC ADVENTURES, WE ROCK!

Here's how you might list your group adventure travel services and for this, you keep it businesslike.

Our Group Travel Services

When you bring your existing group to us, we will make sure you receive the travel experience you had in mind. To ensure this happens we interview you in order to understand your expectations, how you "see" the tour unfolding and key experiences that must be factored into the itinerary you wish to travel. Once we agree on the outcome of your group adventure, we will request a non-refundable deposit and get to work.

Our services include:

- Group rate negotiations
- Value-add negotiations
- Meet & Greet and send off
- Adventure insurance recommendations
- Group leader/guide recommendations and hiring
- Luggage Tracking Apps
- General adventure travel advice
- SOS Apps recommendations and training

Exchanging the Tour Guide Flag for An App

Okay, so you may not be waving a flag around in the woods to attract members of your adventure group, and you may be off the grid and out of cell-tower range. But, there is a feature within the mTrip app called Tour Leader. Here's the info:

Situated directly within the mobile app, tour leaders or organizers have access to a restricted feature which will allow them to:

- Send push notifications, text messages or emails to a specific traveller or every member of the trip.
- Have the location of every member of the trip displayed on a map.

For more information on all that mTrip can do, go to
https://www.mtrip.com/en/tour-operators-travel-agencies/

RELIGIOUS / CHURCH GROUPS

Winning a church group is always an interesting exercise. There's usually someone, who has a spouse who owns a travel agency or who is a travel agent. If this is the case when you knock on that church door, you have two options:

1. Ask if the travel agent mentioned will handle the group no matter what you submit. You want to make sure that your research will not be used by the agent of record.

2. Charge a fee up front to do the investigative research. Secure all commitments in writing before you start.

If no travel agent exists amongst the church group, then you should be up and away and on your way to a decent adventure booking.

Religious Adventures

Not all church groups want to sit inside a coach and tour religious sites. There are thousands of hardy religious souls who would like to get outside and rough it. That could mean traipsing through jungles, to climbing mountains (perhaps for charity), doing volunteer work and even study a religion not their own.

That last activity has always intrigued me as very few travel agents, or suppliers offer a 'not your religion' tour. Why can't a Christian church group experience a Muslim journey? Can Jewish travellers not walk in the footsteps of Buddha? Of course, any of these adventures would attract the outgoing faithful. You may have to go spec' and create the tours yourself.

Generic Church Group Adventures

Off to camp, canoeing the Rio Grande, hiking trails, even climbing Mount Kilimanjaro which has become a church group adventure. The key thing is the church members are travelling together, enjoying that thrill before coming home safely for dinner and also including their prayer time and whatever they need to cover off regarding their faith. It is important to ask about the group's prayer requirements and make the arrangements in advance should certain places require permits.

PHOTOGRAPHIC ADVENTURES

The combination of adventure and photography is a match made in heaven, and it's been that way since the first image was shot on film. To attract the adventurous photographer, search for camera clubs and also any outdoor club, be it kayaking, climbing, hiking or the local community club. Amongst those member lists will be photographers.

Also look for retail photographers who shoot weddings, corporate and family portraits. Then check out all camera stores and ask if any of the staff are outdoor adventurists. Slowly you will build a local list of prospects. Once you have your list, what will you market? How about the BEST?

National Geographic Photographic Adventures
If NG is into this segment of adventure, then it has to be selling. If you fancy this niche why not start selling NG tours first so that you can get to know how they work their magic. NG does pay a commission to travel agents – here's the confirmation email as of March 2018.

Dear Mr. Crowhurst,

*That is correct; we are still taking bookings from travel agents with a commission between 8-10%! If you have any other questions or would like to make a reservation, I would be happy to help. You can reach me, or one of my colleagues, at **1-888-966-8687**, or via email correspondence. I look forward to hearing from you!*

David
Reservations Specialist
National Geographic Expeditions
1155 Connecticut Avenue NW, Suite 300
www.natgeoexpeditions.com

So that's an excellent start right there, wouldn't you say? Now, if you do well in selling NG, then chances are there is no need for you to create any other tour products. Just sell NG and sell a lot of it.

You cannot represent yourself as being part of NG, but you can certainly learn about how they market to attract those photographers. Start by ordering an NG brochure. Check your camera gear too; you are going to need it and possibly upgrade it.

Here's information from the NG website: *National Geographic offers a variety of ways to improve your photography skills with the guidance of a National Geographic photographer. All of our photography programs are designed for amateur photographers of all levels interested in improving their skills. On our photography expeditions, you'll learn tips and techniques while exploring picturesque places with a National Geographic photographer. Also, all voyages aboard the National Geographic fleet are accompanied by a certified photo instructor; and a National Geographic photographer joins every expedition aboard the National Geographic Explorer and National Geographic Orion, as well as each of our European river cruises.*

You can read more at this link:
www.nationalgeographic.com/expeditions/interests/photography/

There are other companies too; you just have to check if they are interested in working with you and if they pay commission. If they don't, have a chat and sell yourself. Negotiate.

http://www.nomadphotoexpeditions.com

Exodus Opens the Door

If you are new to selling adventure travel, but you do have an adventurous streak and would like to capitalize on it, then take a look at what Exodus Travels offers travel agents who book clients on their adventures. Click to: https://www.exodustravels.com/ca/agents and you'll be swept off your feet with their loyalty program. All you have to do is SELL! Okay here's a snippet, you get to realize a 30% discount and if you sell a lot, well, as I suggest, visit that link and read!

Women Who Shoot

Are you a female photographer? Check out what the extreme ladies are doing regarding adventure photography? You may not be selling these types of adventures, but you can watch and learn and scale it down to suit the level of women's adventure photography you would like to sell. Click to this link – it's eye-opening.

https://www.outdoorjournal.com/focus-2/insights-female-adventure-photographers-part-1/.

Showcase Your Own Adventure Photos

Dig deep for your first adventure photographs. You can use them in your marketing. The image below was taken on my trusty Brownie 127. That's me in the center of the insert – an arrow points to the Brownie. As mentioned previously I hung out over a 3,000-foot drop to get the shot. Those were the days!

ADVENTUROUS ART GROUPS

Just like those adventurous photographers, there are adventurous artists who will lug their easels, brushes and paints or sketch pad, pens and pencils along trails, up mountains and down rivers. They are eager to capture the various landscapes as they see them.

Knowing this, what's your next step? Well, if you are an artist, professional to amateur, you could be looking at your next niche adventure market. Like all the other common interest groups, there will be an artist group waiting in the wings for you to meet with and sell an arty adventure.

One of the most famous wilderness artists is Bill Mason, a Canadian. Here's the information about him. When you read about his life and what he accomplished you should find more than a few ideas on how to package your art and adventure programs. Watch his movies/videos too. https://en.wikipedia.org/wiki/Bill_Mason

Climbing Artists
Just caught an article in a 2016 issue of Climbing magazine that showcases the art of climbers who like to get to the top and sketch. Here's the link: https://www.climbing.com/people/8-climbing-artists-you-should-know/

Locating and Promoting to Art Clubs
Your next job is to start searching for art clubs with an interest in painting outdoors. This is called Plein Air and the activity is centuries old, dating to the French Impressionists. There you see, you have something else to mention in your marketing. Keep it 'plein and simple'. Promote: *Plein and Simple Adventures. Leave those four walls for the outdoors. Come with us and paint the world you see.*

Secure a Local Artist
If you can secure a well-known local artist to go along on your adventures and to offer advice, that's another value-add you can promote. After the trip why not host an art event and showcase the works produced by your adventurous art group? It will attract and could build more clients for your next art in the wilderness trek.

THE ADVENTUROUS CRUISER

Cruising is now a mass-market vacation. There are low-cost cruises, two-for-ones, cruises to nowhere, repositioning cruises and world cruises. The cruise niche fits all budgets from a few hundred dollars to half a million. In between all of those ships, schedules, itineraries and gourmet dinners are one or two adventure cruises that can become a niche-within-a-niche. It could be your next niche.

From Large to Small Boat Sailings
How big is the most recent new build? Royal Caribbean's Symphony of the Seas is now the world's largest cruise ship at 228,081 tons. It will carry over 6,000 passengers, a couple of thousand crew and "it has a lot to offer" the media release says. If anyone of those passengers needs a little excitement in the adventure department, the ship boasts a zip line.

It's that or selling a voyage on a sailing boat, a motor vessel, even a sleek white yacht that can go where the big ships can't. Want to sell journeys up the Amazon, Snake or Columbia rivers? You can. Alaska? You bet.

If you are not yet familiar with small boat adventure cruising, then search online using that very term. In the mix is Adventure Smith Explorations. They love travel agents and even have a sales manual you can download. Check it out here: https://www.adventuresmithexplorations.com/small-ship-cruise-travel-agents

Attracting the Adventure Cruise Client
There comes a time in every luxury cruise passenger's life when they have eaten enough Baked Alaska and simply crave a ham and cheese sarnie or even better, a meal cooked over a campfire. To attract those pampered cruisers, you could challenge the luxury lifestyle and pitch that it's about time they sailed 'for real.'

Now it's important not to denigrate deep water luxury cruising. That's not the game here. You are going to compare it to something more down to earth. Smaller, more intimate, more adventurous and quite possibly more exciting.

THE CORPORATE ADVENTURE GROUP

If you manage a corporate travel agency or operate a niche that services corporate travellers, you have a chance to introduce something new to set their hearts pumping a little faster than usual.

There's a caution to be mentioned here. It is something I learned from experience – and it wasn't a nice one. I worked for a corporate agency, and we were pitching an account with the idea of arranging an event. An adventurous event. I suggested a river rafting trip, and that's when the client side went silent. Who knew? We didn't, but I guess we could have if we had dug deeper. As it turned out, this company had lost one or two of its executives on a river rafting expedition the year before. I can tell you; you never forget those moments when the floor falls from under your feet.

Moving along – there is a healthy business to be had, arranging soft adventure trips for corporate teams. Now, here's another lesson to pass on: as you may know, corporate teams come in all shapes and sizes. Some people cannot physically enjoy certain events/adventures. Learn it now, that you must sit down with HR and discuss who might be attending such an adventure event and work your magic to include everyone.

There are tried and true land-based events that do include everyone, and they are fun to do and will involve the entire team. There are companies who set up these events and they will work with you if you bring them in to be the event supplier.

The adventure might last a day, a few days, over a weekend or be gone for a week. Typically, it would be a staff bonding adventure or simply a let's get crazy few days. The activities range from surfing, rock climbing, backpacking, mountain biking, hiking and plenty more.

Creativity Is the Key
What most corporate accounts are looking for is someone to take on this project, come up with great ideas for the adventure and bring everyone home safely for dinner. It is okay to ask the client what they want then turn it around and respond with something beyond their expectations. Build on what they tell you. Sell insurance if heading out into the wilds.

THE INCENTIVE ADVENTURE GROUP

You can bet this incentive will be based on sales, production or something to do with generating profits. The people involved would normally be Type-A go-getters, and that means they'll want to be challenged.

When you chase after and win this type of incentive group, or a client brings the event to you to plan, you can release your inner creativity, go all out and set up a challenging event. It could be a 5-day hike through the mountains or a one-day river rafting expedition, a kayaking trip, a mountaineering jaunt or a combination of all of them. Ideas here: http://www.incentivemag.com/

The client company will usually take care of the internal workings and administration of the incentive. They will come to you to arrange the outdoor component. Let's say there are ten winners from various branches of the firm. They could be earning six figures and would probably lead a pretty nice lifestyle. You might want to keep that in mind and either arrange for the adventure to end in luxury or keep it down and dirty and in tune with the adventure itself.

Caution: Separate Flights

If all these top movers and shakers are from the same company, never book the entire group on the same flight. It is an inherent rule. The reason being if that aircraft crashes, the company has lost its entire top selling/executive team. This rule applies to all corporate accounts.

The Incentive Niche

The incentive niche is a demanding and lucrative niche. There are well-established firms who have been doing this for years. If you are a single IC or a small agency it could be a tough road to haul. But, on the other hand, if you develop a specific niche such as – for women only, there could be more than a decent return on the time and money you invest.

Let's come up with a title you could use. How about this one:

WINNING WOMEN

Travel Incentives for Executive Women

You can change the word 'executive' to whatever word you wish. It might depend on your target audience. Although some companies offer incentives to all staff, when it comes to rewards like travel, they tend to focus on the more senior people that produce revenue.

Search online for Incentive Travel companies and explore how they market themselves, the words and phrases they use and the programs and services they offer. Make a list of what you like about their approach and then reconfigure to suit your own ideas. I suggest you also make contact with these firms and ask if they work with travel agents. Many do.

This link might help you get started:
http://www.becomeaneventplanner.org/index.html

THE WINTER ADVENTURE

It would seem from a recent study I read that close to 80% of Americans are interested in taking an overseas trip during the winter. Now that's a promising start to your Winter Adventure Niche, isn't it? The next line suggested that just over half of that 80% are motivated by the winter weather. Better read into that comment: cold, crisp and sunny. Not so much wet and miserable. But then, you never know!

There's a host of winter festivals and events you can choose from. China's Harbin Ice Festival is one. Then there's watching caribou herds migrate. If your clients have the big bucks, they can get to the North Pole, go ice fishing with Inuit guides or relax in a hot tub and stare skyward to watch the Northern Lights dancing in the sky above them. What will it be?

Winter Research
Time to do your due diligence and find out which countries offer the best winter adventures based on snow and sunshine with an allowance for one or two miserable days. You can look to any of the Northern Hemisphere countries and then go south. Antarctica has seen a boom in visitors. The numbers are heading towards 40,000 if the trending continues.

From skiing to snowshoeing, to kayaking to visiting ancient sites, peering into volcanoes, sleeping in ice hotels and perhaps navigating the Northwest Passage with Eyos Expeditions. www.eyos-expeditions.com

Although their websites may not state the fact, most of these book direct adventure firms will work with travel agents. You may have to negotiate, but then that's all part of the business. You are in sales, so sell them on the fact you can and will deliver.

Winter Sun
To some of your clients, a winter adventure might be interpreted as trekking somewhere nice and warm when it's snowing, rainy and windy at home. Another niche-within-a-niche. Think about places that offer winter adventures to pump up the adrenaline without the need of a parka. I guess that means Australia. Winter here, summer there. Hiking in the bush might be one adventure to offer.

THE WELLNESS ADVENTURE

I'm going to liken 'wellness' to exercise, healthy lifestyle and the fact that more and more people are attending yoga classes, tai chi and making lifestyle changes, losing beer guts and more. When you target this group to sell them an adventure, an obvious inclusion would be food and exercise.

Most adventures would be exercise enough. However, this group may still want to visit the gym at the end of the day. There's no harm in staying in shape for the adventure to come.

Cycling, kayaking and hiking are laced with exercise. When the group stops for that BBQ, better consider whether to use organic or not. Chances are, the answer to that question would be yes.

Is Wellness an Adventure?

For some clients leaving home is an adventure. Depending on what the wellness package/tour includes, the 'adventure' could be arriving in another country, travelling to a gorgeous spa to exercise and eat right.

Now, the wellness theme could be happening with wildlife walking past your client's room or tented accommodation. Next day add a soft adventure component such as a Big 5 safari. We could change the definition of soft adventure and go with: *"Take me out and thrill me, but bring me home to the spa, alive and well."* You can take it from there.

The wellness niche is all about North Americans changing their lifestyle and eating habits. If you can turn that trend into a wellness adventure niche, you will have business from within that 5-mile radius.

Wellness means exercising your rights. Then your lefts.
In the end you'll be totally reconfigured.

Travel Bliss

Wellness and Travel enjoy an inherently co-dependent, symbiotic relationship. The act of travel, of getting out of your standard routine stimulates the endorphins in your brain to double-down on producing joy and happiness-enriched feelings. And wellness, which affects every single aspect of one's being; the mental, the physical and the six travel senses (seeing, hearing, smelling, tasting, feeling and, of course, the sense of humour), feeds off those ultra-positive travel endorphins. Suggesting that this is a winning combination is an under-statement. But going one step further (to use a travel analogy), the sensual pleasure of Umami – a Japanese term often used to describe absolute culinary satisfaction – intertwines with travel and wellness to showcase the reason why so many people seek experiences that recharge their human batteries. Fresh air, fresh food, a fresh outlook on life and the development of personal connections with a destination; this is the recipe for travel bliss.

Steve Gillick
Active Ingredient, Talking Travel

Thanks to Steve Gillick for giving me permission to reprint his thoughts on wellness and culinary travel bliss. I've inserted this between the Wellness and Foodie Adventure pages as a transitional page.

THE FOODIE ADVENTURE

Eating is an adventure all by itself. When you have to trek for miles to finally get to that table, then that would truly be a foodie adventure. I recall hiking in the English countryside then making for a pub where a plate of bacon and eggs, fried tomatoes, toast, jam and a cuppa tea finished off the adventure nicely. But what about today? Where's the adventure in the lure of fine food?

When you think about it, you could, if you are a foodie yourself, construct a soft adventure around the food or foods that you so enjoy. There are also typical foods served at typical restaurants in your city that are the gateway to foodie adventures. Allergies aside, everyone eats pizza, sushi, Italian, Chinese, Indian, but then, is it authentic? Shouldn't they be heading to the place where they can taste the real thing? Answer: yes.

How about heading to China to hike the Great Wall (away from the tourists) and then settle down to a home-cooked meal. Let's then head into the foothills of the Himalaya and dine there after a trek. I'll go one more: how about a kayaking adventure down the River Wye in Wales and pulling in at each pub along the river bank?

Sailing holidays and docking at small villages along the way for the local fare is a good choice, too. Barging along European canals, the same thing. Stopping to purchase local wine, cheeses, meats and fresh bread. I can taste it all now. Then there is the actual cooking school adventure which ties in local walks and hikes to taste not only the food but the culture and the countryside. There is even a specialty training program for culinary travel professionals. https://www.worldfoodtravel.org

Take a click to https://www.epitourean.com/ccts/sign-up and then over to https://www.savoredjourneys.com/. Both websites have something to offer you and would make a great place to start. Reach out and chat. Find out how you can work with companies like these. Ask if they will book your group, pay you a commission, give you a tour seat to go along with your group.

THE BIRDING ADVENTURE

Although birding is mentioned briefly in the trending reports, it is a major activity that falls into the soft adventure category. I'm including it here because photographing birds is a passion of mine, plus there are suppliers who specialize in birding tours and countries that boast hundreds of species. Chasing those birds will take you and your clients to some wild adventurous places on the planet.

In 2013, the U.S. Fish & Wildlife Service claimed there were 18 million active "away-from-home" birders who traveled at least a mile to see birds. Another 41 million were stay-at-home "backyard birders". Other resources place the head count much lower. None the less, the numbers are impressive and to me indicate opportunity. The obvious next step for you, if you like this type of activity, is to look for birding groups in your neck of the woods and approach them with a selection of birding tour ideas.

Books, Movies and Destinations
There have been some wonderful books written and movies made that include birding as the theme. Albert Ross is Lonely by Anthony Dalton is a wonderful short story and the movie Rare Birds starring William Hurt is excellent. Both the book and the movie feature a specific species and destination and that's one of the keys to selling a successful birding tour. You have to know what's flying, when and where.

Birders with Binoculars and Cameras
It's important to know which client you would like to chase. There are birders who like to watch and record the species they see through their binoculars. There are bird photographers and then a combination of both. Whichever profile you end up selling to, they would be heading to the same destinations inhabited by certain species and the specific bird the group or individual wants to record or photograph.

Don't Wing It!
It's never a wise thing to wing anything especially when it comes to birding tours. People who follow this activity generally know their stuff. This means that you should match their knowledge or work with someone from the birding community who can keep you on the right flight path. Search local birding clubs for someone you feel could serve as your advisor.

Promoting Your Passion

My favourite bird to photograph is the White-Tailed Eagle. I have hundreds of images and one or two would lend themselves to being printed as a promotional poster, such as the one below. Don't be afraid to use your own images to promote your tours.

Birds of Prey to Hummingbirds

The range of birds is amazing. From birds of prey to seagulls, to hummingbirds, to finches, to ravens and the thousands of birds sporting multicoloured plumage – you have a wide and varied menu of birds and destinations to work with.

What's It Worth?

You could peck away at selling local tours and then you could set your sights a little higher and attract your dedicated birding clients to something grander. Try this tour from Field Guides: Antarctica: Antarctic Peninsula, South Georgia & the Falklands. Dates: Feb 14 - Mar 8, 2019. Price: $16,950. Duration: 23 Days. Pax: 15. Now that is a nice bit of business right there. https://fieldguides.com/bird-tours/antarctica

Places to Go

There are books galore that will lead you to the best birding locations worldwide. Explore online and also at your local Wildbirds franchised store.

Humour Can Work Too

A little humour can go a long way – perhaps as far as where our Toucan can be found: from Southern Mexico, through Central America, into South America and south to northern Argentina. Here's one idea:

MORE TO EXPLORE HERE

http://naturetravelnetwork.com/birding-nature-tours/tour-company-classifieds/

http://www.wildbirds.com/Find-Birds/Bird-Tour-Companies

https://www.americanbirdingexpo.com/the-birders-directory-travel-issue-released/

https://wingsbirds.com/

http://www.10000birds.com/

DEEP ANCESTRY (DNA) ADVENTURES

If you enjoy those ancestry programs on TV, then you might just like this adventure niche, which is: helping your clients arrange an ancestral tour. Usually, this would mean your clients have either completed a DNA kit and mailed it in to National Geographic or Ancestry.com, received their results and now know how they arrived at where they live.

If they combine a genealogical study with their DNA ancestry results, they will have the makings of a fantastic adventure as they trace or hunt down their relatives. Those relatives could be overseas, on the next island, down the road or still sitting where their ancestors always sat.

The map below shows the migration patterns over thousands of years as people followed the food, the weather, the coastline and eventually, again over time, walked, rowed or sailed to where they decided to set up home.

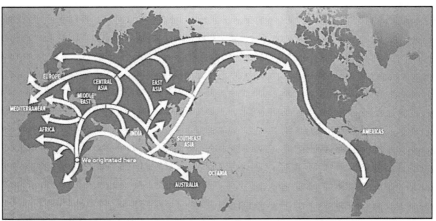

From my DNA kit: The National Geographic Genographic Program Map

I have completed two National Geographic DNA programs, and the latest version tells me I am 46% English/Irish, 40% Scandinavian, 11% Western and Central Europe and 3% Central Asian – and I love it all!

If I was a client of yours and you specialized in this Deep Ancestry niche, then you would be planning my adventure to the UK, Ireland, parts of Scandinavia and who knows where in Central Asia. That sounds like an exciting niche to service.

With more research via DNA we could whittle it down to a town. You never know, we could also whittle it down to a few cousins on the edge of the steppes. A trading town along the old Silk Road. Isn't that exciting?

The Dual Career

Another opportunity. A dual career is staring you in the face with this niche. You could become a genealogist and marry that expertise to your travel knowledge, and charge fees for tracking down ancestors and then earn a commission when booking the trip.

There's more on this topic in my eGuide Ancestry Tours, and you can preview this guide from my website www.sellingtravel.net.

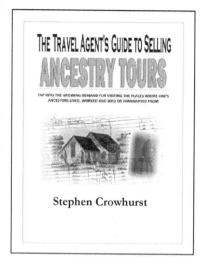

Start with Ancestry.com

One way to get the feel of this lucrative and fascinating niche is to trace your ancestors. There are one or two free sites but Ancestry.com has invested millions to source the records, and they are the actual documents. You can save any of the documents to file and store them for future generations. I am personally back to 1816 on both Ma and Pa's families and have visited a few graves, too. Give it a try and decide if you would or could be the ancestor detective/travel agent.

Left: My grandfather sitting on his rock in 1913 at Power Glen, St. Catherine's, Ontario. R: Me sitting on the remains of his rock 90 years later.

OFF PLANET ADVENTURES

For some reason, I've always had an interest in space tourism. It would seem to me to be the number one adventure of anyone's lifetime. Sure, some people prefer to have two feet firmly planted on Planet Earth, but, wouldn't it be an adventure to head out into the universe and look back to see where you live?

Millennials Say Yes to Space Tourism

According to a new Pew report, about 63% of Gen-Yers or, Millennials say they are up for a space vacation. The most common reason given for wanting to go was the desire to do something unique. Well that's good news. Here's a future niche in every sense.

Fact is, space tourism for space tourists is not yet ready to take off, despite about seven companies in the mix attempting to get their versions of a space adventure up and running. But you do have something close to space travel to sell those gutsy Millennials. It's called a zero-gravity flight and operated by Zero-G. Here's the information from the Zero-G company website – click to the link for more.

$4,950 + 5% tax: One seat on a weightless flight to include 15 parabolic maneuvers creating 20-30 seconds of weightlessness each. Includes ZERO-G merchandise, pre and post flight catering, professional photos of ZERO-G Experience®, video of weightless experience and certificate of weightless completion. https://www.gozerog.com/

The Pan Am Lunar List

The Pew report suggests that Millennials are the first generation most interested in space tourism. Well, they must have forgotten about the Lunar List that Pan Am built. When the airline announced galactic flights, they had a surge of inquiries. People signed on, received their card stamped with their number in the lineup for seats. Total space tourist wannabees reached well over 90,000. The first flight was scheduled for 1987. Looking back, 1987 was slightly premature.

Are You Ready?

Are you ready to sell adventures into space? Will space tourism ever happen? Well, in someone's lifetime it will. Perhaps yours. Right now, you can think about those Zero-G flights.

If You Have the Money

If your clients have the money, meaning millions, they could and probably would book direct. But you never know! Back in 2001, an American businessman paid $20 million to ride with the Russians all the way to the international space station and back. His space adventure lasted eight days. That man became the first space tourist. Since then, there have been six other space tourists. **Newsflash!** On September 18, 2018, SpaceX announced a Japanese businessman and six invitees plan to charter a privately funded moonshot. Launch date: 2023. Not quite the first tourist into space as claimed, but hey, good on them for trying. Click to this link for more information and a listing of the companies targeting space tourism. www.popsci.com/how-to-become-a-space-tourist#page-5 https://www.spacex.com/

Close but No Cigar

In the late seventies, I took a deposit on a space flight. A young couple paid a $200 deposit for their friend's newborn to be air born come the time space tourism was legit. We typed up a document that stated the deposit was to be put towards the first tourist flight into space. A few months later they returned to ask for their money back. The thought was there! Shortly after in the early eighties I connected with Shimizu Co., of Japan, a company planning hotels in space. Nothing built as yet.

It Will Happen Eventually

If this niche excites you, keep watch on the topic. There are adventures you can plan around the concept of space travel such as hiking what looks like a lunar landscape.

Spaced out and ready to go SELL!

This just in. Orion Span is planning to offer agents, $50K for selling a seat worth, $9.5 million. https://www.orionspan.com/agents

GLAMPING ADVENTURES

I include this outdoor combo of glamour and camping because it is showing up as a niche. Glamping aka Glamourous Camping – for some of your clients might be the "adventure" to tack onto the end of a real adventure, soft or otherwise. You could always suggest that after a harrowing trek through parts of Africa for instance, your group gives in to a little pampering? Still in the wilds. Still possible to view wildlife only in a more glamourous setting.

Types of Glamping

The following intro is taken off the Glamping Hub website: *From barns and cabins to tree houses and caves, there are all sorts of types of glamping. You'll find each one described below, along with a link to start browsing through each one. While each of them is unique and distinct in its own way, you can count on unique structures and an incomparable access to nature.* Click to this link and view what's available and check out their video.

https://glampinghub.com/types-of-glamping/

FEATURED ACCOMMODATIONS

Here's a great Glamping Hub video to share with your clients.

Now, I don't like to boast, but I think our tent pitched at a camping resort near Calpe, Spain, should have won the prize for: The Best Erected Tent with Laundry Lines Attached. Sadly no one looked our way. Regarding provenance – you can see we were into our unique style of glamping so early in our adventurous lives. Did I mention this housed four men? Enough said.

There are a few things you'll need to do, set up, create, read, think about and get, before you can start marketing your adventure niche.

Here they come.

MARKETING
TIPS, TOOLS, TECHNIQUES
AND IDEAS

FIRST THINGS FIRST – PREP & PLAN

Before you can start marketing yourself and your selected adventures you'll need to do some homework and prepare a marketing plan that is supported by a well thought out strategy. This strategy of yours will include many things such as photographs, video, a bio featuring your adventure history, copies of any articles written by you or written about you, magazines you plan to publish, books you plan to write, the supplier's products you intend to promote and sell. You'll need an ad & promo schedule and a budget for eighteen months that includes your travels, social media activity and more.

Okay, that's a heavy burden to bear right off the mark, BUT, it has to be done, or you'll be running about here and there, getting nowhere.

The following pages contain tips, tools and marketing activities that are suited to selling travel, and based on my personal usage. As you read on you will discover many more ideas yourself, and that's how you will build towards your marketing plan.

What follows assumes that you are an IC or operating a small travel agency. I make that statement as the ideas, and the tools I suggest are low to no cost. Larger travel companies can more or less buy the expertise they need versus DIY.

I'm also assuming you are new to selling adventure travel and possibly new to selling travel, period. Apologies if I am "preaching to the converted," but I have to start somewhere regarding imagining a readership.

One more thing for you to plan and prep for is your own adventure schedule. It is imperative that you build a list of adventures you have experienced and intend to experience. Keep it local or go around the world. Just make sure you have some adventures under your belt and planned in the short and midterm. It will all help when you start to promote your adventure provenance, past, present and future. Consider inviting your clients to join you on those future adventures.

ATTEND ADVENTURE TRAVEL TRADE SHOWS

I'm going to start here and recommend you attend local to national adventure travel trade shows. Both trade and consumer. No matter where you live, chances are there is an adventure travel show planned shortly – or it might have just happened. It may not be scheduled for your city or town, but it will be booked into the closest largest city. Check out event listings online.

Your first attendance will include listening, learning, chatting with suppliers and with consumers. When you engage with either, there is no room for stumbling and fumbling. Make sure you know the questions you'd like to ask suppliers and the questions you would like to ask consumers.

When you question suppliers, you'll be asking about what's trending, where are the adventurous Boomers travelling to, how about Gen-X and Y? Ask about trending destinations too, facts and stats, marketing support. Keep it businesslike.

When you question, or rather survey consumers, you'll be asking why adventure travel? What's the pull? Where to next? When? Get an idea from the consumer's point of view as to how they feel about adventure travel. Hand them a business card and simply say, *"If I can be of any assistance in the near future, please call me."*

After you know what you need to know and handled a few bookings, then you might be ready to purchase a booth at one of the consumer trade shows. Once you've honed your trade show skills you could buy a booth at other consumer shows – shows like Lifestyle, Fitness, Wellness and so on.

Create Your Own Trade Show / Event

If no adventure consumer shows exist in your area, create your own. Don't be shy of putting on your own adventure event. Check with your preferred suppliers and ask for funding and participation. Keep the event small and intimate if you wish. Focus on clients and their adventure friends – or, go the more expensive route and advertise the show to attract adventure prospects. Also, ask your suppliers for advice. They have been there and done this and know what works and what will be a waste of money.

You might find that outfitters and retailers who sell adventure gear versus travel are very interested in supporting your show or perhaps sharing a booth with you at the well-established adventure and outdoor shows.

Travel and travel gear go well together. There will be local to national retailers ranging from Eddie Bauer to MEC to REI to Blacks to your local outfitter. Contact them all and talk up the fact that you service the adventure client. They might offer ideas from their event marketing history (if you ask) and decide to work with you.

For coaching on how to put together a trade show, visit: http://thetradeshowcoach.com/

Notes:

FOUNDATIONAL TOOLS

There are tools, gadgets and devices that are part of your everyday life that you will turn to good use from a marketing point of view.

One thing for sure is this: you cannot be using an old clunker for a phone. You will need to upgrade. As I mentioned I'll be writing about what I use and how I use it – I have an iPhone 7 Plus. Your phone should at least shoot 10 MP images and 4K video. If not, then you need to upgrade. Click to this link to read about the latest and best rated phone cameras. This was published before Apple released it's XS. So, check that too. https://www.techradar.com/news/best-cameraphone

Next is your website. Is it a clunker too, or is it a finely tuned beast of creative genius? If your website is not up to par, then it must be updated. The updating has to be done before you open for business. No point in opening your doors physically or electronically if you do not have the tools in place to support your business going forward.

How's your social life going? How many social media accounts do you have? One, two, six? Probably, for this enterprise having more than Facebook, YouTube and email is overkill. However, if you are a social media whiz, and I am referring to marketing, then chances are you will have the time and energy to factor in one or two more social tools such as Instagram. Always a good idea to research which social media your core client/generation uses.

Remember, time is the challenge. Time is the beast to beat. Twenty-four hours a day is all you get. Same for everyone. Some people manage to accomplish a lot in those 24 hours, others barely move. It takes planning if you intend to make good use of your day.

Here's what I use to create my marketing and promotional content:

Phone Camera	DSLR Camera	Photoshop Elements
Scanner	Printer	Graphics Source
Animoto	The Logo Creator	Snag It

IMAGES AND VIDEO CONTENT

Let's start with images and video content. The reason for this is simple: without quality images and video you are not going anywhere with your marketing. No one will be inspired by a fuzzy image or shaky video. So, it's important NOT to shoot first and ask questions afterwards. Ask the questions first and then shoot.

Selfies

Guaranteed you have a ton of selfies somewhere on that phone of yours. The question is: are they the right type? If not, that means you must get busy snapping yourself on location with suitable backgrounds.

Like me, you've seen the mug shots some travel agents use for the 'me' shot on their social media accounts. Same goes for their About Me webpage. I can recall more than a few "look at me" images that would send a creature of the wild crashing into the jungle! No need for low cut, high cut, chest hair, speedo or any other form of revealing attire. Keep it businesslike. Near naked attracts the wrong type of adventurer. On the other hand, you might have stumbled upon a new niche.

Your Best Side and Angle

Here's where you put some time into shooting selfies from various angles to make sure you capture yourself in the best possible light. It doesn't take long to analyze which is your best side and the angles to shoot from. Always be aware of that half an arm in the image when shooting a hand-held selfie. Use a tripod, a phone bracket and learn how to crop your selfies using the editing tools in your phone or your photo editing software in your home computer.

If your nostrils, jowls, top of head, chin are taking over the shot, then the angle is not correct. Work at it until you get it right for you. You should end up with a decent ten to fifteen selfies that you can use to post to your blog, use on your website and social media and also insert into your publications. If your phone offers portrait mode, then learn how to use that too.

Here's some of the kit I use when shooting selfies:

I use several Gorilla tripods and a RetiCam phone clamp. The RetiCam is solid and will not drop your phone over the cliff. Professional selfie sticks are heavy duty, and some come with a Bluetooth button or handheld remote to take the shot. They also have a tripod adapter built into the handle and a gimbal that keeps your phone level.

RetiCam

This accessory is well constructed, and up to any adventure you put it through. It does require an equally strong attachment to a tripod or selfie stick. You can purchase it on Amazon.

Pro Selfie Stick

The stick shown here is one of many. It's holding a GoPro camera where your iPhone would sit. You can see the tripod threaded end of the stick, and the handheld remote. Buy on Amazon or a local camera shop.

GorillaPod

I use a small one for my iPhone and the larger version for my DSLR. They stand firm and wrap around tree branches, poles and posts. You can curve it to use as a selfie stick and shoot without an arm in the picture. Buy from Joby.com.

The Selfie Video

Okay, now we're getting serious. You are going into the movie business, and YOU are the star. Video as we know it is outstripping static images when it comes to selling travel and especially adventure travel. The same thing applies to selfies. Your adventure clients would just love to sit back and watch you hiking, standing atop the mountain and rushing through whitewater and this is how you should be promoting yourself.

Just as you must build a bank of ready-to-use selfies, the same thing applies to your videoed selfies. One tip I can give you is not to stop and start but to keeping videoing and crop later. Another tip is to repeat the "take" just like Hollywood. Take One! Nope. Take Two! Almost. Take Thirty! Got it. Maybe. One more time. You understand then, that shooting video selfies takes patience and perseverance. Better if you can have a buddy behind the camera to manage the video shoot. Keep it as real and as basic as possible. The end result should be natural. You can top and tail the final cut with intro and exit FX's, but don't let the effects override the adventure content.

The Video Rig

Whether you use your iPhone or iPad, you'll want to keep your camera steady. Fuzzy, shaky videos will not sell you as intended. Using a video rig helps stabilize the camera and produce a much better video.

Here's one version of a video rig, very similar to the one I used. They are quite cheap to buy. However the plastic casing on the cheaper versions is flimsy. Better to go with a more robust model. Along the top, you can see three cold shoes where you would slot in a mic, a flood light and any other device. This rig sports a level which is a nice touch.

The current smartphones have upgraded their cameras and lenses however if you felt the need to expand on them, there are more choices in the lens department from zoom to wide-angle. I caution again that this is all about videoing YOU doing what you are selling. That means keeping it natural and basic. Too much or too many effects will ruin the production. These rigs start around $30 and go up. You can buy them online.

Whatever rig you buy make sure when your phone or tablet is inserted that you have access to all the buttons on the edges of your device. I found some rigs cover or impede use of buttons on both my iPhone and iPad.

Using a Video Rig.

Imagine you are hiking through a forest, up a trail, coming out into the open to stand on a summit and then look around at the vista. You would be holding your video rig in front of you, moving it (slowly) to the side, to the ground, stopping to film an insect, flower, bug, bear (!) or deer and then moving on to sweep (slowly) across the horizon. That's the basic footage, and now you set the rig on a tripod, and go sit on a rock in front of the camera and chat with your viewers. Hold that pre and post video pose and smile for a few seconds before and after so the video can be edited to start and finish with a great smile.

When you lead a group, have all members sign off on a release, allowing you to film openly without worrying about who should or should not be in the video. This release form should be included in all tour registration documentation.

Your Video Voice

Here's where scripting and practice beforehand pays off. We are at the stage of preparing to launch your adventure travel business. There are many things to do before you say, "I'm open for business." When you do open your doors for business, you'll want to be off and running, not stumbling.

Try videoing yourself chatting to the camera and an imaginary audience. Then watch and listen to yourself. Invite others you trust to listen to you talking on camera. Is it just okay or is it fantastic? Is your voice sounding thin, whiny, boring, monotone or is it full of life, resonating well, captivating? The sound of your voice is VERY important. People will not watch and listen to your video if your voice is too harsh. You will lose business. What to do?

The answer is to take voice lessons. Learn to speak on camera, how to move and how to look into the camera. Learn how to move from one comment to the next and practice these important transitions until you do it naturally. You could hire in the talent, but better if it's you – in person.

Video Editing

We are spoilt with software and apps for editing both images and video. Some of the software programs require that you be a Hollywood level editor. You do not have time for that level of program. Best to select the easy but good software. Adobe Premiere Elements seems to top the list as the easiest to learn with enough bells and whistles to get the job done. If you still have access to Microsoft's Live Movie Maker – that was the easiest. Luckily it still resides in an old laptop of mine for when I need it. Remember this is all about promoting adventure travel, not showcasing your movie-making talents. Beware: editing programs are seductive, and you could end up editing all day long and not marketing.

At this stage, you should have a folder full of selfies, video content and now you will need another image folder full of classic adventure imagery that you have taken or have permission to use by whoever owns the image.

Warning: If you didn't know, the images on Google Images are not free to use. Most professional images online are tagged and can be traced to your website or wherever you use them. You may not hear anything for a while but at some point in the future an invoice will arrive – and the amount will be big, large, huge!

You are encouraged to shoot your own images and source directly from suppliers and tourism boards and be sure to obtain written confirmation to use them. There are image banks online that allow for corporate/business use. All they ask for is a donation to the photographer or a line of text under the image that credits the photographer or website.

With your ready-to-go images and video clips, you will be able to populate your website, your blog, your vlog and post to Facebook, YouTube, Instagram and anywhere else you intend to promote.

Here's another reason to study videography: check out this call for adventure videos by ATTA. It was in my inbox recently.

Calling All Adventurous Films

Do you have a short film that inspires adventure travel? The fifth annual Adventure in Motion Film contest has begun and is currently open for submissions. If not this year, try next year. Check it out here and learn the rules: https://www.adventure.travel/film-contest/apply

YOUR WEBSITE – THE ADVENTURE HUB

Let's move on to your website – the HUB of all your marketing activity. Back to basics we go. If you do not yet have a fully functional, widescreen scrollable website with a mobile version that plays in a vertical format on a smartphone, then you are waaaaaay behind! Time to kick your own butt and smarten up and get that website up and running ASAP. If it helps, I use Weebly: www.weebly.com. It is user-friendly, affordable, and you control everything.

Your Adventure Marketing Hub

If you are an IC, your website is the equivalent of a street-front travel agency window. If you are that street-front travel agency, then your website is a digital version of your agency and your agency window. Either way, your website should be engaging, functional, exciting to visit, offer adventures of a lifetime and should nudge the visitor to BOOK.

You might read or hear that when it comes to social media – you must not sell. You should only engage, chat, socialize. The suggestion is that you take it easy, no sales pitch, take time to build a relationship and so on. It all makes sense, but while you are playing nice and socializing, your book-direct suppliers and sales minded competition are social selling and moving past you. Closing more sales. Your sales.

Inform Your Clients What to Expect

When you develop your client base, you inform them through your marketing that you use social media to promote your best adventures and your special offers. When your viewership, readership, existing clients and prospects understand how you do business you will attract the clients who want to book, not just chat. In the end, you must decide how you intend to make use of social media, your website and any other marketing outlet you use. In my book – you use them to sell.

Your Website – Where All Things Converge

Whether you use your website in this way, or not, a website is supposed to be where all your media converge. It is also where prospects and clients alike, remind themselves about your services, location and how to contact you. It is also where those same prospects and clients click to check out the adventures coming up, scour your blog posts and play your videos.

Your website is or should be your marketing hub. I know that social media is always rising to the top and that's a good thing. However, when it comes to business basics and marketing at the level of a one-person travel business or a small retail street front agency, your marketing tools will be your website, email (still the number one tool in the digital toolbox) and at least one, perhaps two social media accounts – Facebook and YouTube.

You will read many reports on the benefits of other social media networks. Acting on some of those suggestions will run you ragged all day long as you socialize when you should be monetizing. Monetizing is the digitized word for selling. If you meet someone who seems to know a lot about communicating through social media, compare them to this man, Brian Solis, who created The Conversation Prism. If your social media gurus cannot speak at this level, then you could be on the wrong track.

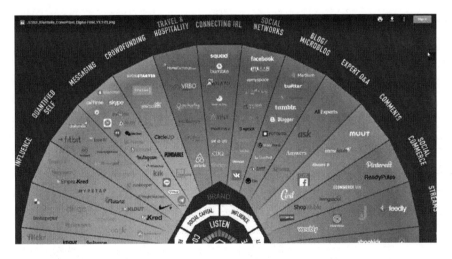

The full-colour version of this image is available to download here:
https://conversationprism.com/

The Conversation Prism is dynamic. Updating from version 4 to version 5 Solis and Szymanski removed 84 companies, added 141, and created four new categories: messaging, crowdfunding, travel and hospitality, and connecting IRL (In Real Life).

Whatever you do regarding marketing, unless you work behind the scenes as a social media guru, blogger, analyzer, crypto bitcoin counter…you will always route your client back to your website unless there is an option to make direct contact via email or on the phone. In other words, at your level of doing business, promoting and selling travel, you only require the best basic tools. Try to make use of the two-hundred or so sites found here: https://en.wikipedia.org/wiki/List_of_social_networking_websites and you will work yourself into an early grave.

KISS Me!

Keep it, what? That's right, Simple. You know the drill. KISS is sometimes very hard to do when you read the travel news each morning, and there it is again, social media being touted as a must do. Facebook for everything. Well, there's a Generation named Y that dumped Facebook four years ago. Who is on Facebook? The good 'old' Baby Boomers. Bless 'em.

Ask the Question

When someone berates you for not being a social media whiz kid, you must ask the question, "So how many bookings have you generated this year over Facebook, I'm guessing a thousand?" Then sit back and wait.

Of course, there is always a leader in all things, and I love those that just do it and make it happen. So, yes, there are travel agents who have worked their magic via social media and closed a ton of business. It's like a few travel agents generating a six-figure income when the average take-home pay for most TAs is around $40,000 or less. There is always someone who exceeds the norm.

Sales generally come from perseverance, never giving up, continual prospecting, being able to see and sense opportunity and doing something about it such as marketing the right product, to the right people at the right time. You can use social media for that too. Once again – be sure to advise your social followers that you use social media to promote yourself and your adventure travel products.

Go for the Low Hanging Fruit

Managing your website, email, and two social media outlets will allow you to do it all. If you want to add a blog into the mix, go ahead. But, you'd better be able to write a few thousand words of WOW content every week. How long will that take? I can tell you from experience – a full day, or two if you want it to read right and be the best there is. No need to make it harder to attract prospects and close existing clients. Every new marketing activity will eat into your prospecting, marketing and selling time – and we haven't made a booking yet. That's my take on it. Just be sure you leave enough time to sell, close, book and follow up and repeat the sequence.

Here are a few more highlights from previous adventure reports. Although some numbers might have moved slightly up or down, the data is still worthwhile taking note of.

- Adventure travellers are younger than non-adventure travellers.
- Overall, average age: late forties.
- The average length of a soft adventure trip is ten days.
- 54% of travellers plan to participate in an adventure activity.
- 42% of travellers currently participate in adventure activities.
- 73% of adventure travellers plan to take another adventure.
- 22% of adventure travellers plan on repeating the same adventure.
- 45% of adventure travellers plan on using a tour operator.
- 78% of adventure travellers use Facebook.

Adventure travellers read publications such as:
- National Geographic Magazine
- National Geographic Traveler
- Men's Health
- Cosmopolitan
- Vogue

The following pages will offer suggestions on how you can market to the adventurous client. I've listed what you should study, learn and read to be better informed about the historical side of adventure travel. Knowing your roots and the history of those long-ago explorers will add spice to your marketing.

Turning Your Website into an Adventure Hub

When I think of adventure, I think of National Geographic. Maybe you do too. And if so, you do that because they have entered your mind via TV and their fabulous magazine and a series of adventure books. When you click on anything NG related it is the BEST in quality, and this is the level you want to emulate. Just like the NG website, when an adventure travel prospect lands on *your* website they should be blown away by the layout, the images, the videos and the action.

Your website must be functional, deliver the best imagery and have several call-to-action statements. Most of your online/offline marketing will push the reader to your website, and that's why it must be the best it can be. Revamp your website to widescreen 16:9 and offer these additional, easily accessible features:

Newsletter	Blog	Image Gallery	Video Gallery	Reference
How-To	Where-To	Supplier Product	Links	eBrochures
Email links	Contact info	About YOU	Newsfeeds	RSS
Consumer Page	Survey Page	The Where to Next Page		
Contact Us	Live Chat	Skype Sessions		Ask Me Now Link
JOIN OUR ADVENTURE LIST SUBSCRIBE TODAY!				

Double check that your marketing content will drive your existing and prospective clients to your website. Once there, they will either be a fan, or they'll fade away. They need something of interest to see, read, be asked to do and to get them involved.

Convert a Visitor to a Lead

A lead is only a lead and a prospective one at that. Even existing clients, who have booked with you before, need a nudge every so often.

When you have too much YOU and not enough THEM, you will lose the customer. If what you have is AWESOME then your visitor might stay long enough to read, scroll and become interested enough to make contact. One great image and one heck of a slogan and you could be filling every seat of your next ten adventures.

Your Website Marketing

Remember your website should be the mirror image of your agency and the agency window. To an IC, a website IS their agency and agency window.

Your About Me page should be the place where prospective and current clients go to read about YOU, your provenance, your skills, your services and from that page link to the agency's social media platforms. Those social media platforms will also link back to your website.

Here's a basic outline of how your website factors into your adventure marketing. At the core of your marketing activities, it will be connected to your social media outlets. I do suggest a digital magazine that you publish each month or each quarter. Your About Me page has to be promoted, along with your blog if you write one. And under *other* comes your product and more.

In addition, the client that has been wooed to your website should find something of interest to nudge them into making a call, send an email, walk-in or acknowledge your marketing in some way or another. Instruct them as to what to do next. The best form of acknowledgement is a booking.

Remember:

Depending upon the location of your agency, your agency window will be looked at and glanced at a few times to several hundred times each day. If you are not facing onto a main street of a major city, or you are working from home, then your website must become the digital equivalent of that agency window.

When a client or prospect clicks to your website, you will want them to be excited about landing there. The visuals they find on your website should be stunning and the text captivating. They should find offers and deals and links to access your articles, your e-magazine, your eBooks and novels.

If this works as intended, your clients will be well informed and ready to book. Make visiting your website the equivalent of peering through the glass of your agency window. They'll become enraptured by the exotic places pictured there. Do the same for your social media too. All roads lead back to your website – even from your social media sites.

GET YOURSELF A LOGO

All those brands you sell, have a logo. It's part of their brand marketing strategy. Their logo has to appear wherever potential clients will see it. That means magazines, online, on the side of a touring coach, airplane, tote bag, iPhone cover, t-shirt, book cover and on billboards. Almost forgot: on their company website too. You must do the same with your logo.

The logo you will create or have created will be current, cutting-edge, FX'd or even retro, vintage and nostalgic. However your logo turns out, it has to be easily recognizable. It should attract the type of clientele you have planned to target for your specific adventure niche.

You could settle for your agency name or your name as the logo. If you go with a text-based logo, then use a particular font and colouring. Create a tagline to support your logo and help sell your services.

Let's explore a couple of fonts for the word, Adventure. As this book prints only in grayscale, you'll have to research online for the best adventure colouring to suit your choice of font. Here we go:

Adventure
Font: Cambria

ADVENTURE
Font: Impact

ADVENTURE
Font: The Dead Saloon

Ginga

Metal Macabe

You Murderer BB

trashco

Roof Runners 3

ADVENTURE ✅

Beyond Wonderland

Scream Real

ADVENTURE ✅

vtks Deja Vu

adventure

To me, the two checked fonts look more than adventurous.

Pricedown

adventure

The choice is yours. Just be sure to explore as many fonts as you can.

Sniper

Font: Yozakura

Font: Adventure

Font: CF Peru

You can find the first two fonts, Cambria and Impact in your MS Windows /Word font list. The Dead Saloon is found at www.dafont.com.

The other fonts are available from a website called, 1001 Fonts. If you visit here: www.1001fonts.com, you will discover hundreds of styles that might just suit your logo, name and the type of adventure you would like to sell. Beware of using a "feminine" looking font to attract female adventurers. Stick to the fonts that turn your name and logo into something any adventurer would be attracted to. Strong, out there, bold, stable and exciting.

When you explore the current offering of adventure company logos they are not too outlandish, and only a couple might nudge you to investigate the company. Most of the fonts are clean, bold and visible Here's one that grabs your attention. It must be the bright green and the black brush splattered background! You'll have to click here to get the benefit of the colour scheme: www.marbleziptours.com/packages/

While you are on their website, check them out and see if you can include Marble Zip in your adventure offerings. Thanks to Marble Zip owner Martin Flynn for permitting me to showcase his logo.

If you can factor in the imagery of someone, preferably you, doing what you're selling then that helps the prospective client move closer to making the call. Stay clear of promoting an empty space. That's okay for one or two shots, but add at least one person, a client, a group of clients. Show someone enjoying what you are selling. The analogy for promoting an adventure with no one in the picture would be a new restaurant promoting its fantastic new dining room and dining experience – and it's empty! Doesn't make sense. Best to take the promotional shot on a busy night.

To create logos, I use The Logo Creator 7. It takes a few clicks to understand how the platform works, but give it an hour and you are all systems go. You can buy the basic creator for under $50. After that, you can select a variety of add-on graphics and elements. They cost under or around $30. Very affordable. Not only can you create a logo, but you can also create promotions, social media headers, and you can use your own graphics too. Subscribe for USD$12 / month or buy as you need.

Here's the link where you can explore TLC7 and the new Web Graphics.

Creator: https://www.laughingbirdsoftware.com/

Here's a promotional statement I created using TLC7:

Check out my FREE ten-page guide to using fonts:
https://issuu.com/smptrainingco/docs/art_of_the_font_a_special_guide_for_travel_agents

Create a Beyond Text Only Logo

You can use TLC7 for more than a text-based logo. Something a little more artistic to represent your adventure travel writing, publishing etc.

Here's a logo I created for myself. I use this one when I'm promoting my photography that I've turned into an art form.

Your adventure travel writing logo will help readers identify your work. When you read about publishing your own digital magazine, you will better understand the need for a colourful logo.

Here's an easy to create logo for a surfing promotion. Again, created with TLC7.

One more idea – promoting YOU in the local community, but selling adventures worldwide.

GET YOURSELF A QR (QUICK RESPONSE) CODE

There are many points of view about the use of QR codes and the majority suggest the code is dead and buried. The negative reviews are more often written by those who are not selling travel for a living. The QR code is a great tool for travel agents. If you've never scanned a QR code before now's the time. Grab your smartphone, use the camera, hover over the QR code below and see what happens.

You've visited my website, yes? Easy peasy. So now imagine you have a QR code on everything that a customer might see and be able to scan. They scan and go wherever you send them electronically. Your QR code can be linked to your website, a web page with an adventure promotion, a sign-up page to join your blog or newsletter and a whole bunch more – hey how about linking to your Facebook page or your YouTube channel?

There are fancy QR codes available but do not get carried away with the fluff. Stick to the clean lines, easy to scan version like the above code. These codes look great on the back of a t-shirt with a message above it that reads, SCAN ME! I suggest on the back as it could get slightly contentious if you are a woman and the QR code is on the front of the t-shirt. No need to set up a situation with passers by aiming a camera at your chest. Try your hand at creating a QR code here:

https://www.qr-code-generator.com/

SHOOT THOSE PROMOTIONAL SELFIES

It's a tough job, but someone has to do it. Your adventure promotions, your About Me web page, your full-screen website homepage and social media headers should all, at some point, showcase YOU. And you can add to that, YOU doing what you are selling.

My usual caption for this shot is, "Here I am working from my outdoor office..."

Photo credit: Mike Tsirogiannis

When is a selfie not a selfie, but acts like a selfie? Yes, there are times, such as this photo of me in my kayak that has to be shot by someone else. A shot like this removes the arm or the bloated too-close-to-the-lens face.

Always carry a tripod or a Gorillapod so you can set up your own "selfie shoot" for both stills and video. When you shoot video by yourself, remember to set up the camera/tripod then walk away and around so that you walk into the frame. You can crop the footage later. If you end with your face in the viewer, make sure you smile for an extra few seconds otherwise you'll end up with a 'final face' you won't like. An extra few seconds of smiling or yahooing, gives you extra cropping time to end on the best fade-out image.

Create a Selfie folder and add more titled folders with labels such as Me mountaineering, Me smiling into the camera, Me running from a bear. Make it easy to find what you need when you need it.

Promote your Group Gatherings

If that was you in the picture below, and that was an excited adventure audience, two things should be happening: someone would be shooting images of you on stage from various angles – I'm thinking twenty shots at least. The second thing going on is the videoing of the entire session. Once again you can edit and crop once the video is complete.

As you can see in the photo, I am not using any AV gear. Just me and the audience. That's okay for some events; however when you are selling adventure, you should default to a 10' screen and fill that screen with dynamic images that have the audience on the edge of their chairs and ready to book.

The Muku Shuttr Remote

One selfie gadget you will need is a remote-control release so you can click and shoot your selfies from a distance. There are hundreds of remotes to choose from – I use the Muku Shuttr which works for my iPhone7 and iPad Pro. Canon and Nikon have their remotes for DSLRs. When you are shooting at a busy street location, there's always that fear as you walk away from your tripod and camera that it won't be there when you turn around. A long, thin, nylon line tied to your camera/tripod is a precaution you might want to take.

ONLY YOUR BEST SHOTS WILL DO

Every image you upload to your website and post to your social media outlets must be of the finest quality in every way. The image should be sharp, and it can be sharp even when the resolution is low.

A blurred or fuzzy image, unless that is the "look" you are aiming for, will cause visitors to click away from your website. I use Photoshop Elements to edit my images. It sells for around $100 and less when on sale. You can check locally to purchase or go direct to Adobe.com. You might consider the Adobe Creative Cloud where you subscribe at $10 a month. Your call – however, the tools offered through Creative Cloud are high end, meaning you'll need time to learn them. I find Photoshop Elements is quick, easy and resides in your computer versus online. If you lose your internet connection you can still complete editing that image.

Always Shoot with Your Website in Mind
When I'm out taking photographs, I combine panoramic, square and regular sized shots. In some cameras you can select 16:9 – the same shape as your TV or widescreen monitor, meaning your image does not need to be cropped to suit the current 16:9 sizing of most media screens.

Shoot with Your Digital Magazine in Mind
Shoot portrait mode so that your image will plop right into a magazine page without too much cropping if any.

Low Resolution
Best to upload and post only low-resolution images as there are some nasty types out there scouring the internet for quality high-resolution images to capture and resell. A low-resolution image of around 100kb cannot be used to enlarge and print by the image bandits.

Protecting Your Best Shots
If you wish to protect your images, tag them and embed watermarks. Store your best of best shots in a separate drive that never goes online. Transfer the image you want from the offline drive to your working computer via USB. That way your best shots remain safe. Also print a hard copy of your very best shots.

VIDEO IS KING

Video is ramping up more views than static images. YouTube, Vimeo, Facebook and recently Instagram's vertical video announcement are all supporting the growth of video as the number one promotional tool. Video is the BEST media type for marketing travel. Facebook is still a small-business favourite when it comes to video marketing.

Here are a few recent facts and stats from Social Video Marketing Community to ponder over:

85% of small business stated video media has won them new clients.
66% reported that video received more likes, shares, comments.
91% plan to create more Facebook videos going forward.
74% plan to create more videos on Instagram.
60% plan to create more videos on YouTube.
63% of respondents paid to advertise a video on Facebook.
29% of our survey respondents have paid for videos on Instagram.

Of the two, Facebook and Instagram, Facebook is still the leading video advertising platform for small business brands. We'll have to assume travel agencies and suppliers are included.

Facebook continues to dominate social media.
50% of respondents said Facebook is their most important channel.
91% said they plan to increase Facebook videos.
63% have paid to advertise their video on Facebook.
43% of them primarily use the Boost button to expand reach.
57% of them primarily use Facebook Ads Manager.

A growing number of businesses believe Instagram has a major impact on their bottom line.

73% said Instagram is important to their business.
74% said they plan on creating more videos for Instagram.
57% have posted on Instagram Stories.

What Social Platforms Are Saying

Facebook advises that mobile consumption trends lean towards shorter, more precise messaging, so publishers should look to deliver their promotional messages **within 15 seconds.** One report gave this advice. It is crucial to your video marketing success.

"People watch videos casually and on the fly – and they rarely turn their phones sideways to do it."

Vertical vs Landscape Viewing

A few things to consider for travel videos. Vertical viewing is promoted for the busy, on the go set and as I ponder the issue it is true, most people I see carry their phone in a vertical hold and view it in that same position. When it comes to viewing travel videos, the full experience comes only from viewing the video in landscape. That sunset, that skier taking off, that mountain vista, can only be truly experienced by turning the phone sideways. And, chances are, the travel viewer will be sitting still somewhere and wanting to view the video in the best format.

So, the information is excellent, however before you accept it and go with it, think about how a client would want to watch your video. The quick 15-second promo can be presented vertically. The full-scale sales video featuring your next adventure would have to be viewed landscape. The 15 second vertical, as the gurus advise, is excellent for your initial recipients to send to their pals. Remember, viral is the keyword.

15 second promo viewed vertically

Full video viewed in landscape

EMAIL MARKETING

Assuming you have completed all the prep work, let's start marketing with email. Email as I recall someone saying is still the #1 tool in the digital marketing toolbox. With that, I totally agree. We'll start here with email and how you can use it to market your adventure niche.

Although email has been part of our lives for the last 45 years or more, it's good to check if we are using it correctly. If you know you need to refresh your email skills, sign up for a local one-day email marketing course. Spend the day and about $150, and you'll be raring to go.

The Mailing List

It's the engine that drives your marketing. It's the heart of your email marketing success. Easy to say, tough to get. Tough to build. So how do you build an adventure client email list? Well for one thing: NEVER BUY A LIST. I can tell you from experience as many other travel professionals will confirm – most of the available lists are junk and when you do use the list you purchase, you will quickly find out that none of the people you are emailing have given their permission to receive an email from you or anyone else. That puts you squarely in default of the spam gods.

Right. So, lists you don't buy. Now what? The answer is this: It's down to good ole slogging, in both a traditional and a digital and social media sense. In essence, you are going fishing. You will use various lures to attract would-be adventure prospects to sign up, join, click on, register, commit to and type in their email address, check the "I accept" box and submit. That's ONE new prospect you have permission to send an email. Next!

What's the Attraction?

Why would anyone type in and send you their email address? Simple. They are interested in what you are promoting, and they do not want to miss out on the next trip, special deal, event or whatever it is you have posted.

The offer of a simple newsletter or access to your blog can result in a flood of email addresses. What is the attraction? It could be you, could be your fantastic photography, a video clip from the last adventure group you ran, and it could be that you're the only adventure agency in town.

Start with Your Current Client List

I'll assume you have a current client list and that's a list you already have permission to contact so we can jump right in and send this list a promotional email that announces your adventure trips and groups and at the same time, ask each recipient to refer their adventure-loving friends.

You may wish to attach a link to an awe-inspiring video clip that your current clients can send viral for you. Keep the clip to something "doable" by all, not hair-raising to scare would-be soft adventure prospects running for the sofa.

Two key words: permission and viral.

Always make sure you have permission to send and always ask the recipient to help you build your business by referring their friends and forwarding your email to others.

Which Email Account to Use?

Another lesson learned the hard way. Here's hoping you can learn from my mistakes and not become one of North America's top spammers. Yes, it happened to me.

I was email marketing from my Outlook account using my local internet provider. Suddenly my email service is cut off. Somehow, I had entered a no-go zone. Too many emails going out. Somehow, a clever rascal tapped into my account and sent thousands of emails without my knowing. Yes, I had anti-virus and internet security software. Long story short: use an email service such as Mail Chimp or Constant Contact. There are others, but these are the two I have used personally.

These email services manage your account, so this type of event does not happen – and if it does, they can track the infiltrator and delete them. Thus, saving your email soul from being blacklisted and unable to send email. Yes, those were dark days for me. But not for you.

Choose your preferred email service, set up an account and make sure you take the tour around the program you are buying. Practice by sending emails to yourself so you can see first-hand what the graphics look like and how the overall promotions would look to a recipient. Some graphics tend to wander out of the frame, so you'll want to select a service with a strong background in travel promotions.

Affordability

I know money is important to independent agents working from home and so your best bet, from my experience is Mail Chimp. They offer a FREE account for up to 2,000 subscribers. See below.

Forever Free Pricing

You can send 12,000 emails a month to a list of up to 2,000 subscribers with MailChimp's Forever Free plan, though a few features are only available to paying users.

https://mailchimp.com/pricing/

I can tell you one thing, as an IC you will never use up this FREE account. If you have 2,000 active clients, then you are obviously doing well over $2 to $5 Million in sales. Sending 12,000 emails a month – would mean emailing something worthwhile six times each month.

So, for the price, Mail Chimp has your back. And they have next level pricing when you wish to get a whole lot more for your money.

The starting price for Constant Contact is $15 /month for 500 subscribers.

There are free trials so be sure to test both services and also click to the link below for additional services you can review.

https://www.top10emailmarketingservices.com/

Emailing Basics

We've been using email for so long we should know the basic tenets of email etiquette and how to use it effectively. Here's a basic primer to keep you on the straight and narrow.

- **Write a clear subject line.** Forget being too fancy, too clever. If the recipient cannot understand the subject line or there are words used that spam programs look for, then you've wasted your time and effort.

- **Add your adventure signature.** Keeping it real, you would sign off with your name and title. The title could change to suit your current status and or promotion. You could be the Adventure Consultant, or the CEO – Chief Excitement Officer. Just make sure the signature statement ties into the email itself. Using MS Outlook, you can create signature templates in the program. Go ahead and create two or three you know you will use on a consistent basis. The one you select as a default will populate each new email.

- **Use a standard / professional greeting.** Unless you are on a one-to-one friend basis with your client, refrain from, *Hi Ya! How's it going today then?* Try, *Hello Steve*. Or, *Hi Steve*. For the more formal, there's nothing wrong with, *Dear Steve*, and then launch into your message.

- **Don't tell jokes.** Humour is great; jokes often kill the message and the messenger. Refrain from, *"Did you hear the one about the...?"*

- **Spell check and proofread your email.** Not just the message but the email addresses (you might have two client names the same) and your signature.

- **Will your client know what you are talking about?** You cannot assume they will. They are busy. They have a life. Explain why you are making contact.

- **Establish a reply time frame.** From a client's perspective, the worst response is no response. Always respond, even if it's only to acknowledge receipt of the client's email. And do it immediately if you can. Let the client know you are working on their request.

The Outlook Email Window

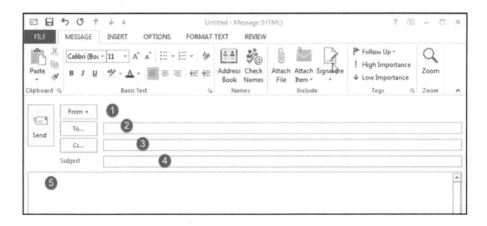

1. Use your adventure email address and suggest your clients add your address to their email white-list.

2. The To: line is meant only for the email address of those who are meant to read and respond.

3. The Cc: line is meant only for the email address of those who are meant to read and NOT respond.

4. The Subject Line as mentioned should contain a clear and concise inspiring comment, a reason to read further, a captivating call-to-action.

5. The body of the message goes here, starting with a professional greeting / salutation.

Setting Up Group Email Folders

Using your email program, set up activity group lists in the Address Book, or Contacts area. If you create these groups from the start and add to them as each new client joins your list, you will save yourself time in the future.

When using a program such as Outlook, you should know that when you populate the To line with a group folder containing several email addresses, everyone receiving the group email will be able to see the email addresses within the group. All they have to do is click Reply All, and every email address within your group folder can be read and that becomes a privacy issue. It is best to use the email services of Mail Chimp for instance which will send your email to each person on your selected list without exposing other email addresses.

https://mailchimp.com/help/create-a-new-list-group/

Here's how your lists might appear in the Outlook address book or in your email provider contact list.

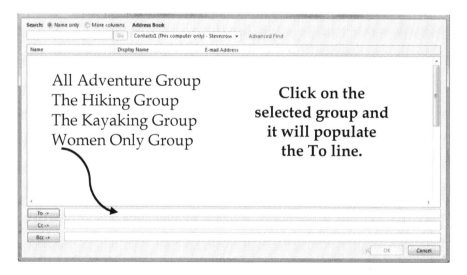

What Are You Going to Email?

Your clients do not want junk. They want exciting information that relates to their adventure interests. Learn more about what your clients want to receive from you, and send it. That does not exclude them from receiving hot news about something totally different to what their core interests are.

Here's a smattering of what you can send, attach and include:

- Links to your website and web pages
- Links to your YouTube and Facebook videos and image gallery
- Links to your newsletter
- Links to your latest blog post
- Articles – text that populates the message window

- Reminders
- Explainer videos
- Audio files
- PowerPoint full-screen presentations
- Puzzles
- Invitations
- Suggestions
- Digital Magazines
- PDFs
- Links to adventure travel books
- Maps
- Special Promotions
- Social Media posts
- Contests
- Updates on adventurous world events, current and historical

One of the key things to understand when using email as a promotional tool is the fact that no one wants to receive huge files or anything that could contain a virus, such as an image. Your name will be mud if dozens of your clients have to battle a virus from one of your emails.

Keep it simple. Send links.

To support your email campaigns, you'll want to first and foremost link to information found on your website. Always to your website – the very hub of your adventure travel business.

On your website, clients should have access to your videos, your digital magazines, your blog posts, a gallery of images. In fact, your website should support everything listed above.

The next step in the process is the creation of what you want your adventure clients to read, watch and listen to. The links you send out should open the best of the best regarding articles, images, video and graphics – with well written CTAs or Call-To-Action statements. I prefer to think of CTAs as Call-To-Adventure statements.

USING SOCIAL MEDIA

Just as you had to promote your business to attract a list of email addresses, the same applies to generating likes, hits, clicks and followers.

I go with the advice one travel guru stated and that is to use one, perhaps two, social media platforms and learn them well. Better to be a professional at using Facebook and YouTube versus mediocre to lousy using five or six social media outlets. You may wish to use Instagram and Twitter. That's fine. Go for it.

Selecting Your Reach

Whichever social media you use, you will want to boost your post so that you spread the reach of your post and stand a better chance of attracting adventure loving clients to become subscribers.

From the get-go you should know that 60% of your Likes etc., will be from people who do not intend to travel let alone climb a mountain. Social media is a strange world and a world where many non-travellers hangout. They join, sign up and take your time, but they are never going to travel. You must be diligent in policing your social media followers and delete the ones who show no signs of life.

This culling takes time. It means clicking on the Facebook page of each LIKE and reading their posts. Any signs of adventure travel photos? Any chat about their recent kayaking trip? No? Then delete. Trim your social media followers to those that mention travel and specifically adventure travel.

The Social CTA

Make sure you advise your social media followers that you use Facebook and YouTube to promote the latest adventure trips you offer. Advise that if they join or subscribe, they will be receiving posts about new trips, best pricing and reports of your adventures. Focus on social selling more than just chatting to pass the time of day. Think about your social CTAs.

- We're going to Kathmandu. Come with us!

- Just back from hiking in the UK. You'd love it!

- Check out the latest video from a client who…

- Watch this client shoot Grade 4 rapids and survive!

- This month's Adventure Magazine just published.

All these CTAs would be a hyperlinked to your website and the page where the information, imagery or video resides.

As you build your social media following you can move into live presentations on Facebook for instance. Perhaps you could even present on location? Here's a Facebook mock-up with a post that talks up a recent trip to Patagonia.

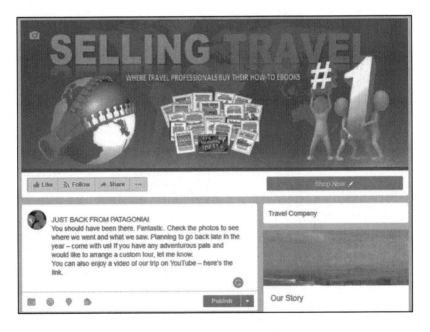

When you add a post like this, remember to support it with images, video and links to your website *for more information.*

At the end of the video, you should be on camera saying, *"Don't forget to book your next adventure with me!"* Also, it's a good idea to invite the viewer to join you on your next adventure, *"Join me on my next adventure to Bosnia – I know you'll love it."*

Use Twitter as the Adventure Unfolds

The world is Twitter mad. That said, it could be one of the best platforms to use when you wish to market on the go. By that I mean when you are on the road by yourself or with a group. You can Tweet from where you are, what you are looking at and support your Tweets with images, video and links to your website.

The concept is to have your Twitter followers, follow you! For instance: Climbing a mountain? Tweet from the Peak!

Let your Twitterites follow you there and back and all the way to your Facebook presentation once you return.: Use hashtags: #tothetop. Check out this "Follow the expedition..." example below:

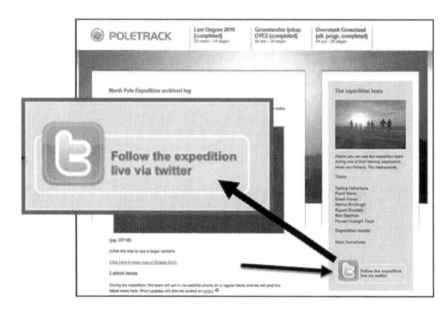

Now ponder this: you are wading through a swamp, up to your neck in alligators and the Swamp People are nowhere in sight to help out. Whaddya do? You TWEET! You send a message about your predicament, you've shot a selfie, eyeball to eyeball with a large 'gator and you post it. Now THAT'S exciting.

- Next, after you make it out alive... you Tweet.
- When you set up camp... you Tweet.

- When standing on top of that mountain... you Tweet.

Now you are building a following with excellent use of images and video to support your Tweets you'll be attracting your next group who want to experience what you mentioned in your Tweets.

You don't have to be leading an expedition. However, your kayak adventure down a raging river, your climb to the summit, a hike along a wild trail will do the trick. As long as you are out there and reporting back live as it happens, you will attract a following. When you return home, you can then target market and plan your next group outing into the wilds.

Instagram

I read somewhere that close to 50% of Instagram users, look there for new destinations to visit. They are relying on information posted by other users. If the stats are true, then you should be posting here and adding a caption to your images. The caption will help the viewer think about visiting. The words you use are important. No use stating, Gobi Desert and leaving it at that. You must add a compelling statement after the title. This is the lure that will nudge the viewer into contacting you. Remember that your images should be sharp.

Marketing to Generation Z

According to the Digital Tourism Think Tank (DTTT), Gen-Z represents a quarter of the population, and in two years, they could account for 40% of consumers. Gen-Z also approach social media in a different way compared with the previous generation. They give high value to privacy and prefer apps like Snapchat and Whisper.

Even more interesting is the fact that 25% of this generation abandoned Facebook in 2014. This is because Gen-Z spend most of their time looking for content on social media instead of social networking. Also, apps like YouTube and Instagram are preferred for video. We are in front of a generation that doesn't only share things but creates things the report stated. Additionally: Gen-Z can be defined as 'curators,' they want to contribute to the conversation and be part of it. That would make them great spokespersons for your agency. Check them out here:

https://www.thinkdigital.travel/opinion/gen-z-the-new-destination-disruptors/

Client Succession Planning

Be sure to review and read about each current generation that's engaging in adventure travel. At some point in your career, you will have to upgrade your client base or conduct a client succession program. In other words, as Baby Boomer adventure clients stop travelling due to age and health, you will have to fill the void they leave behind. You do this by appealing to the next generation and <u>before</u> the Baby Boomers leave your client list.

Your client base should include all generations; however 'we' tend to gravitate towards our own generation. They are easier to communicate with because we are them. That said, you need to keep your client base growing and you can only do that by attracting the younger adventurer who exist in the next generation and the one after that.

Check your customer stats:

Review the generational make up of your adventure clients and decide when you should think about a client succession strategy.

Total Adventure Clients: 560

	Number	% of Total Clients aged 70
Seniors		
Baby Boomers	300	25%
Gen-X	160	
Gen-Y	100	
Gen-Z		

I have to assume you maintain full customer information that includes your client's ages and date of birth. If so, then you can review let's say the Baby Boomer category and determine what percentage are nearing seventy years of age. If that percentage is more than 25% then you should initiate a customer succession plan immediately to attract the next generations.

Note: When anything related to your business exceeds 25%, you must factor in one or two safety factors to offset the loss of that 25%. If an account contributes more then 25% if your revenue, you will suffer if you lose them. If 25% if your business comes from one adventure destination, move into another to offset future downturns. Remember, the Power of Three. Spread the risk.

MOVIES, BOOKS AND ADVENTURE TOURISM

As you may know, when an action-adventure movie, filmed on location, becomes a box office hit, tourism tends to increase to that location.

Even movies set in a specific country but filmed elsewhere generates an increase in tourism. The Last Samurai, for instance, was filmed in New Zealand. It had Japanese look-alike scenery that boosted tourism to both Japan and New Zealand.

Keep an eye on what films are playing locally, trending online and sold as DVDs. If there is a destination that has an adventure product attached to it, it is worth investigating. If the featured location happens to be your favourite, then chances are you could ride on the promotion of the movie.

The same is true of books, both fiction and non-fiction. They create a stir when set in a specific country. The Da Vinci Code for one set many tourist groups scurrying around Europe searching for signs.

The book cover shown here is from my bookshelf and one of many books that can inspire your adventure clients to join you on your next trip. You might also use one of the journeys described in such a book to plot a group tour itinerary.

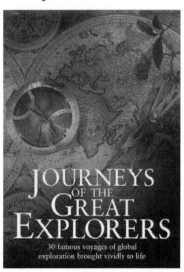

Look for these types of books online or at your local bookstore. These so-called 'coffee table' books are filled with information, maps and ideas you can turn to good promotional use. At the very least, when you come across such an exciting book, mention it in your blog or send an email to your client list to get them engaged and talking about the content of the book. After that, email to find out who might be interested in going 'there' to wherever it was.

HISTORICAL EVENTS

Historical events offer you a series of ongoing marketing ideas. Each year, upon the anniversary of the event you can remind your clients of past explorers and the adventures they experienced.

I've already mentioned the summiting of Mt. Everest when Hillary and Tenzing topped the mountain. Each year there are expeditions of one sort or another heading somewhere that might suit your promotional plans. You can celebrate historical events by escorting your group to that very spot where the event occurred. Shown below is the ceiling of the Pen-y-Gwryd Hotel, Snowdonia, North Wales. This hotel is famous for its signatures, written on the ceiling by such eminent climbers as Hillary himself. Also, John Hunt, Wilfred Noyes and others.

This particular hotel and this ceiling have meaning to all climbers. So perhaps a climbing adventure in the Snowdonia National Park and few beers in the Pen-y-Gwryd hotel afterwards. On a clear day climbing Snowden is a strenuous hike, a soft adventure for sure. In the wintertime it can become a killer mountain. Summer is your season to sell it to your soft adventure adventurer.

I attended a local book fair in early 2018 on the last day of the sale. When I got to the table labelled history, there in the box, all by itself was a 1952 first edition of Man of Everest, The Autobiography of Tenzing. What a find! Cost $3.

In the book, the answer is given as to who summited Everest first, Hillary or Tenzing. According to Tenzing, it was Hillary and then six steps later, Tenzing himself stood on top of Everest. Hillary took out his camera and took several shots of Tenzing holding up his ice axe adorned with flags. That image became the iconic photograph of their climb. The photograph of Tenzing is included in the book.

Look for vintage publications related to your specific adventure. Then, when you host adventure evenings and promotional gatherings you can speak from those books.

There is no short supply of books and journals by past and present explorers and adventurers. They range from hiking to kayaking to climbing to cycling to fishing big game or angling in North American backwaters. Almost every type of adventure topic has been written about, so there should be a book that supports your adventure niche.

PROFILING YOUR ADVENTURE CLIENTS

If you have not yet developed a passion for a specific adventure, it would be best for you to profile or survey your existing client list and find out what type of adventures they are passionate about. If there is an overwhelming interest in say skiing then perhaps this is the niche you decide to promote.

Eventually, something will lead you to a niche that you like, find interesting and then attract like-minded clients. For instance, here's the tail end of an idea I had which involved taking groups to New Zealand to climb and bivouac overnight on Mt. Hikurangi. The reason for overnighting was to witness the dawning of the next day. The idea was based on the fact that Mt. Hikurangi receives the first sunlight of each day before the sun works its path across the Pacific Ocean. It would make for a great New Year's Eve / Day Adventure.

It is possible to create an adventure niche from scratch. All you need to make your idea a success is a few hundred, to a few thousand clients who readily understand your concept and are as passionate about it as you are.

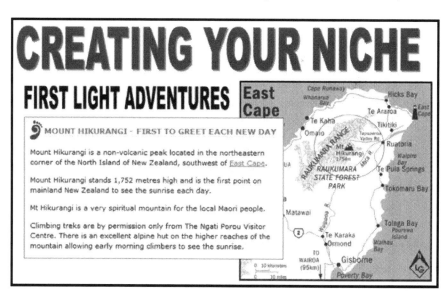

Once you establish a passion for a certain type of adventure, or sell what's trending right now, such as hiking, then you can start to profile the type of clients who will purchase what you are promoting. You can start with your existing client base. They may all be hardcore cruise clients, however in there somewhere is an adventurer waiting to put their boots on.

To Profile or Not to Profile

Profiling your clients depends somewhat on whether or not you have a passion for exploring a particular destination or activity, or you intend to create an adventure niche from scratch. Profiling your existing clients will help you determine *their* level of interest in your personal passion or the niche you've selected from the many choices. Profiling also helps you determine which adventure travel services to offer.

Profile your Existing Clients

Client profiling is something to be done annually, as everyone will go through life-changing events and make decisions based on what's happening to them, today. You must stay in touch and be interested in the adventurous lives of your clients.

- You might find that someone has passed away, leaving their loved one with an empty heart but also with time and money and a need. Many times, that combination causes the person left behind to get motivated and live the rest of their lives to the hilt. With that comes "doing what you've always wanted to do." Going to visit a long lost relative, or climbing that mountain you've dreamed of climbing since you were a kid – and the only thing that prevented you from doing it was the life that came your way. There are so many people in your community in this situation or soon will be.

- You might find that regardless of loved ones passing on, someone has decided: it's retirement time and to heck with everything and everyone, *"I'm going on an adventure!"* – and that's when they reach out to you.

- You might find a group of younger travellers from age 16 to 20, or 20 to 30 – all well connected via social media and wanting to step out and step up, or kayak a raging river, or just roam the world. Even to volunteer their time and energy to help the less fortunate in the global village. They too, need your guidance.

If your adventures are unique, design a profile of the client you feel would enjoy your product versus generic soft adventure tours. Once you have identified your niche adventure client, you can add to your profiling a secondary list of generic soft adventure customers. Your initial niche promotion targets your niche profiled clients. The second promo phase targets your generic adventure clients.

There are various survey methods open to you. There are free services too. Just before we take a look at the best survey methods for you to try, it would be a good time to review the current demographics of the adventure-based client. Once you read through the information (check ATTA website), you'll have a better idea of what to look for within your adventure client base. Note: women are leading the adventure market.

How and What to Survey
Here are a couple of basic but FREE surveying tools and two of the more well-known programs – Survey Monkey and Constant Contact. Check locally for other FREE survey tools.

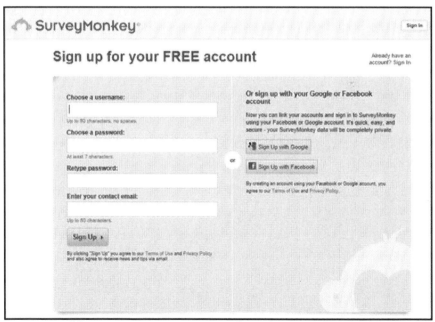

https://www.surveymonkey.com/user/sign-up/?fefla=survale

http://www.constantcontact.com/online-surveys/features/create

Once you find the best survey tool for you, review the various survey question options such as Multiple-Choice questions, Yes or No, to Free Flow responses where the client will type a sentence or two. You'll also have access to Rank and Rate questions allowing your clients to rate something from 1 to 10, like to dislike, bad to good.

The BEST returns would be the RANKING / RATING question as this is less work for you. The Free Flow response means you'll be reading all night long and trying to capture keywords and common phrases to decide the mood of your clients. Too much time. The suggestion is to go with the Ranking / Rating Styled Survey. You could also add in a Yes/No question for decisive answers. Make sure your survey tool counts and graphs responses. Here's a sample of the Ranking / Rating question format:

Rate an Adventure Trip as something you would like to do?

| Not interested | | Would like to try | | I love adventure! | |

What type of Adventure Experience would it be?

Hiking	Trekking	Scuba	Kayaking
Eco	Scuba	Rafting	Caving

You also want to know where and when your clients are thinking of going. You could phrase your questions as follows:

Where in the world would you like to begin?

North America	South America	Europe	Asia
Australia	New Zealand	Other	Other

You could list continents, or you could list only the destinations you serve. You could leave two spots for "other" where the client types in their free flow choice. Usually, the survey tool will list "other" responses, which means you will sift and sort for common responses and total them.

When are you planning to go on your next adventure?

J	F	M	A	M	J	J	A	S	O	N	D

Surveying the travel date/time of year is very important. This information will tell you how and when you should market your products and also when to market and follow up with the clients who responded. Keep your clients focused on the current year and 'next' year. You need sales this year and you need to know what future business you might transact.

Look for Patterns

Travel & tourism is all about patterns. Reading the survey results you realize you have a strong base of clients who already love adventure travel. **The rest would like to try**. The main soft adventure activity to try is **hiking**, and the preferred destination is **Europe** in the month of **July.**

Now you can think about your marketing plan and with this primary data, you can be very specific in what and when you promote.

Timing for the adventure seems to be summer to fall. Now you know you should start marketing in the first quarter of the year. That's right. You must work backwards from the tour date by three to six months for when you should start promoting your upcoming tours. Experience and hindsight is always good – it helps you get it right the next time.

If you needed more marketing time, then you have just learned a lesson. Start marketing nine months out.

Here's how your final chart might look:

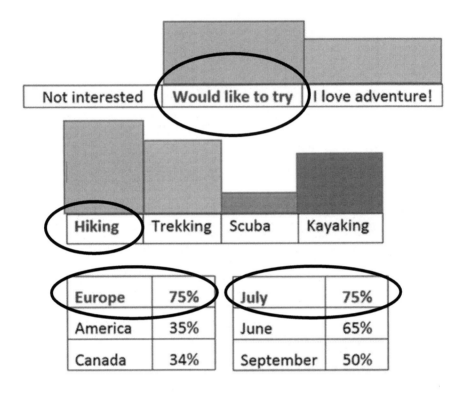

Demographics and Psychographics

You can survey your clients for more information related to their financial status, their postal code, lifestyle preferences and more – even their preferences in coffee! Contact adventure magazines and publications and ask for information on the demographics and psychographics of their readership. Slam dunk. Done in one. Magazine surveys offer the insights you need.

What they do and why they do it (psychographics) is important to your marketing plan. I agree with that, but things change all too quickly today. Nothing is set in stone. Get the information you need and be careful that you do not get locked into old news and miss the current trends. Check the dates of the readership survey.

NEWSPAPER AND MAGAZINE EDITORIAL SCHEDULES

This is a great tip. I picked it up many years ago. It entails contacting the travel editors of the top newspapers for sale in your area that publish a travel section. The same applies to editors of adventure and travel magazines including National Geographic. What you are asking for, and it may be listed on their websites, is the upcoming editorial calendar. The editorial calendar is used by the publication to attract advertising.

The editorial calendar lists scheduled dates, headings and storylines that will be published in the coming issues. Travel sections generally appear in newspapers on the weekend, and most travel magazines publish monthly. Therefore, you will have 52 opportunities x the number of newspapers that publish in your area, to promote when the travel section has been published. Travel magazines publish each month. They give you 12 opportunities each year x the number of adventure magazines.

Knowing these editorial schedules ahead of time allows you to decide what you will promote on the weekend.

Example:

Imagine there is going to be an editorial piece in your local major newspaper featuring adventures in Europe. An outdoor magazine is featuring kayaking in Japan and an online publication is doing a piece on hiking in Arizona. Let's go one more and include National Geographic and let's give them an issue focused on journeys to the North Pole.

Right. That's quite a menu. Here's how you take advantage of these four editorials, articles and focused issues. First things first: your job is to advise your adventure clients about the articles and on the day of publication send out a promotional email selling your adventure tours.

Other things to think about:

- Major newspaper: Who reads it? Baby Boomers – yes. Other Generations: possibly and if so, they'll read it online.

- Outdoor magazine: Who reads it? Those who subscribe to the magazine. They will read the hard copy that arrives to their home, and or read it online opting for the digital, save the trees, version.

- An online magazine: Who reads it? Subscribers and the odd click by. They'll of course read it online.

- National Geographic: Who reads it? Millions of North Americans. Baby Boomers and the elder Gen-X. They read the hard copy delivered to their home. Other generations likely read it online.

Sample Email Promotion:

Email can cover off all generations, all readers and all editorials in one swoop – however, the only people seeing your email would be your existing adventure clients. Message reads:

Hi everyone:
Just letting you know about four inspiring articles appearing over the weekend in the Daily Blurb, Get Outdoors Magazine, Online Adventures and National Geographic. They will be covering (fill in the destinations and activities and here's the most important thing for you to promote) *"I can arrange any of these adventures for you."* Note: don't forget to include the links to the editorial pages.

Facebook Promotion:
Promoting the upcoming editorial via your social media accounts gives you the opportunity to boost your reach and readership for a few dollars. Spend twenty-bucks to reach thousands of people. Use the same message you used for your email campaign.

YouTube Promotion:
Here you can record yourself chatting to your webcam, pitching the editorials and presenting the fact that you can arrange any adventures mentioned in the articles. Don't forget to smile, showcase your email, telephone number and website and add a Call to Action.

DELIVER SOMETHING AWESOME

You have many choices. You can sell the same ole adventure listed in your preferred supplier's brochures, and for some, that's awesome enough. Or, you could work with your preferred adventure suppliers to create what you believe is going be an Awesome Plus Trip of a Lifetime. Then you'll have the pleasure of developing a niche-within-a-niche.

The Niche-within-a-Niche – now that can be a money maker.

You may not have heard this expression before – **a niche-within-a-niche**. What it means is this: within established niche markets there is always another niche, sometimes so well hidden most travel agents miss it. But when you sift and sort and dig a little deeper, you find that golden nugget. Usually, there is someone who has discovered the niche-within-the-niche already, but then again, perhaps YOU are the first to think up the concept. Let's explore:

The term we are using is Adventure Travel. The style or type of adventure travel most agencies sell is called Soft Adventure. Under that heading, there are 20 or 30 activities that a customer can book with you such as scuba diving and hiking and kayaking. Then within just those three activities, there are different spin-off activities.

The idea is to make sure you drill down through all the possible combinations to find out if there is indeed a specialty niche for which you have the knowledge and the background to take on and build into a profit centre.

You can apply the same concept to almost anything travel related. One of my favourite niche ideas is photography. It is a passion for me and also for so many other people, and as you know pretty much any gadget can snap an image today.

If we added photography to hiking, then the location and the preferred subject matter might change. It will depend on what the tour group want to photograph. Let's decide on hiking around Kyoto, Japan. For the subject, we could settle on cherry blossoms, or fall colours, temple roofs and trainee geisha in their kimonos.

Next if you wanted to drill down further to make this hiking tour of Kyoto even more unique, you could decide to attract only those photographers who shoot with a Canon camera. Drilling down one more level, you could even name the model of the camera. I'll name my camera which is now versions old, but here it is, the Canon 40D.

The benefit of naming the camera model (and hopefully yours is more current) is that it will attract photographers who shoot with that specific camera model and then, and this is the big thing, the group can gather and chat about how to make better use of the features of that camera.

If you managed to find an instructor for the trip and he/she shoots with a Canon 40D for instance, you'll have something else to promote. The main closing statement for such a trip is the exchange of knowledge.

A Women Only Shoot
This tour could also be Women Only. A tour for women from all walks of life who love photography and would like a custom tour group just for them. You could approach a local camera club and other clubs where women share a common interest.

Here's how your niche-within-a-niche camera specific tour that includes an instructor might look when you promote it.

A specialty tour for photographers who shoot with a (camera name/model)

Come with us next spring when we fly to Japan to hike and photograph

KYOTO

Bring your gear, share your knowledge and learn from photographer (NAME) as we explore and photograph this magnificent ancient city and hike the hills around it.

Photo credit: Steve Gillick

Recap:

At this point, you have a lot to think about. What we have covered is more or less Step One in the process of creating a profitable Adventure Niche. With this information alone, you can move forward and start to put together your adventure travel content and promotion schedule.

☑ The best of all worlds would be to sell ALL adventure suppliers and also focus on one adventure type, your personal passion or one of the tour products your suppliers offer such as hiking the Himalayan foothills, cycling in France or kayaking white water. Your choice.

☑ You might decide to focus on one country and study it for every possible adventure to be found there, or one type of adventure experienced worldwide. The model for a true adventure specialist.

☑ Your photography skills and the images you produce will support your marketing and your sales efforts. Be sure to start a folder and save your best of best adventure images to that folder.

☑ Read books. Write books. Subscribe to adventure magazines. Join ATTA and other adventure-based associations and groups.

☑ Seek the advice of your adventure suppliers and chat with the BDMs who have travelled extensively. Learn from them.

Notes:

HOW IMAGERY AFFECTS YOUR ADVENTURE SALES

To help boost your readership and adventure travel sales, support your travel writing with your photographic images, video or both.

When you shoot the image or you arrange for someone else to take the photo with you in the picture, it adds credibility to your article. The concept of being there, on-site, as you wrote about your experience has a better chance of being credible when you are actually in the picture. You don't need to be featured in every shot. Just one or two would suffice. I repeat: no need for the UFC lolling tongue or devil's horns hand signs unless that would be relished by your readership.

It is a mistake to say or believe you are not photogenic, or you don't like having your photo taken. It's a must do. No complaints. Learn the craft of setting up the shot and get right into the center of the image. Learn which side is your best side. Study your facial expressions, shoot hundreds of images until you know how you look from different angles. Review your attire and make up. Learn which colour suits your complexion. Now, do you look like an adventure-selling travel agent?

Don't forget the shots where you can have some fun and spoof yourself in certain situations. Readers enjoy good clean humour and a visual joke here and there.

Keep in mind what we are working towards: you as an adventure selling travel agent, writing about your travels to generate more adventure sales. You'll want to be professional in all aspects. Excellent photography will boost your chances of being read. You can expand the idea of photography to include posters, sketches, watercolour, video and enhanced images. Let your creative talents rise to the surface and produce images that sell you and your adventure product.

The image shown below is one of mine. A sketch that I photographed then turned into a poster using the Adobe Photoshop Elements software. The cost of PSE is around $100. Very affordable.

Perhaps you are artistic and like to sketch, too. If so, why not support your article with a sketch – and, if it works for you, photograph your sketch and posterize it or use a watercolour filter. Use your artistic talents in your marketing. Everyone uses a photograph. What if you used your sketches?

You might be a pen and ink artist in which case you are linked to those artists who sailed with expeditions in the 17th century to record the landscape, flora and fauna. The pen and ink artist came before the photographer.

Your adventure clients and your readership will appreciate the fact that you were there and took the time to produce an original sketch. Whichever route you take, the whole idea of supporting your marketing with writing and imagery is one more key to your success.

Reports tell us that today, consumers are more interested in viewing a short video than reading a blog. They want that multimedia experience. And today, video production is as easy as holding up your smartphone and pressing the record button. The video quality is good enough for your intended use which is to add video support to your blog or webpage where you post your adventure promotions. If you publish a magazine on the Joomag platform, then you can insert your travel video so that it plays from the page.

Your Very Own YouTube Adventure Channel

Say it again! Video is KING. Yes, it is. It is the best format for promoting travel and if the number of videos played each day on Facebook and YouTube is anything to go by, well, you just have to jump on that bandwagon. You may prefer another video outlet/app, and that's great. Just remember, the masses view Facebook and YouTube.

Using video as your "visual writing, blogging, vlogging" tool is easy to do but tough to do well. On the other hand, you are not trying to become a Hollywood producer. But, you could think of yourself as an adventure photojournalist travel agent. Writing and shooting images and video to showcase your adventures.

Whether or not video is your number one form of imagery to support your writing, you should open a YouTube account and create your adventure travel channel.

Once your channel is live, upload your edited videos from wherever you are in the world and then email or post to your social media accounts. Post a note to your readership to visit your YouTube channel and to watch your latest video. If you blog, then your video can be embedded into your blog. A link can be embedded into your promotional article or typed out in the printed version. In PDF format, links are live and clickable.

Use video as if it was an email. Instead of writing behind the scenes, you are speaking and presenting in person. Stick to a 30-second sales pitch, just like those advertisers do on television. Be sure to end the video with a link that stays onscreen long enough for someone to read it. Tell your audience when you will be back at your desk. Advise when your adventure show will be on. Invite everyone to visit you at the agency.

Check out each of the eleven channels listed at the link below.
See what you like, dislike and could do better.

11 Inspiring YouTube Travel Channels to Follow

https://theplanetd.com/youtube-travel-channel/

To open your YouTube channel you must have a Google account. Visit www.youtube.com and create a channel by typing in your Google information and you are on your way!

Get Smart: Check your smartphone. Do you have the latest version? Does it have the best-of-best camera and camera apps? If not, time to upgrade.

Use your smartphone to capture your images and video – especially videos of you chatting with locals for instance. Make sure you carry a light but sturdy tripod. Shaky videos will not attract a YouTube viewership.

Shooting the Adventure

If you prefer to video everything, then you are becoming a vlogger. Similar to a blogger, only you do not post the written word, you post the videoed word. Once you get used to looking into the camera and speaking to an imaginary audience, you will enjoy the excitement and speed at which you can create and upload your promos. Shoot every adventure so that you have a bank of clips, ready to use.

If your video is crisp and clear, then you can also isolate the screen and save stills from the same video. Most current video production and editing software programs offer this feature. You can research Pinnacle Studio by Corel.

If you decide to use video as your main promotional tool, then you should visit www.joby.com/store for the tripod and other accessories. You'll need a boom microphone that plugs into your phone or tablet. A set of lenses to attach to your phone's camera helps you zoom and shoot wide angle. If you upgrade, then chances are your new phone has everything you need such as twin lenses for zooming and portraiture. For a sneaky shot of someone in the marketplace, there is a right-angled mirror lens for both your DSLR and smartphone. Referred to as a spy lens.

Using your smart phone as a photographic tool is known as phoneography and you can search online for more information on how best to use your smartphone as your main investigative camera.

The iPhone has its own set of supporters and websites that can deliver everything you need to know about using your iPhone as your main camera. Click to these iPhoneography links and explore:

http://www.iphoneographycentral.com/
https://iphonephotographyschool.com/iphoneography-websites/

Below is my kit for when I am on assignment.

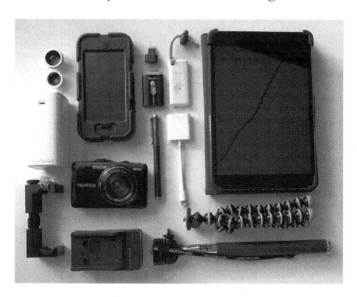

Lenses, power booster, clamps, iPhone, pocket camera, charger, mini drive, pen, remote, iPad, tripod, selfie stick.

Animoto Video Adventures

Another of my favourite programs is Animoto. It is a fantastic tool for promoting your next adventure. It is video based, which means you will be able to make excellent use of those clips you have banked. The basic account is free and the next level up is only $39 per year. I suggest you splurge and buy the $39 account. Animoto is very easy to learn and you can create on the road using the Animoto app. www.animoto.com

Add captions and short sentences to entice your clients to book. Add a sound track from the Animoto library or one of your choice. The last image in your Animoto video should show a link to your website and a specific webpage where more information can be found about the adventure.

Photo Credit: Mike Tsirogiannis

Think of all the ways you can use Animoto to spread the word about your travel writing and your latest posts. Once finished, you can embed your Animoto videos into your website and post them on your social media sites too. Even export them to your YouTube channel.

www.animoto.com

Here's a sample Animoto video I put together for you. It's very short but delivers the concept that you can develop and expand on using your own words, video and stills. Animoto videos can be edited, updated time and again. Type the bit.ly link into your browser to view my video.

http://bit.ly/2p5djlm

Video Site Fine Print

You should be aware of the Terms and Conditions i.e. the *fine print* when uploading your videos to sites like YouTube and Vimeo. There are conditions that allow, in this case, Vimeo, to use your video content. You retain ownership; however, Vimeo is allowed to use your video as they explain.

https://vimeo.com/terms

YouTube has similar terms and conditions. If you do not want your video used in this way, then you must upload your videos to your own channel and check the PRIVATE box. If the public box is checked then everyone can view it. You can be selective as to which video you want seen by a worldwide audience using Vimeo, YouTube or similar.

https://www.youtube.com/static?gl=CA&template=terms

Whichever video outlet you use be sure to read their Terms and Conditions online and make sure their rules and regulations will work for you. Be sure to read terms related to: License to Other Users, Duration of Licenses and Non-video Content

Notes:

CHOOSING YOUR CAMERA

There is no right or wrong choice here. The factors that will help you decide the type and style of camera you choose will be based on the type of images and videos you intend to capture. PLUS, how much baggage and equipment you want to carry.

BOLT Case Cover

Your generic smartphone can actually do it all for you and if you download certain photo apps then you can even edit on the go. Here's my iPhone7 Plus with hard screen protector and hard rubber casing **with a lanyard loop**. The lanyard is very, very important. It will prevent losing your phone over that deep, deep chasm. A lanyard also prevents theft.

Your smart phone can produce both quality images and 'snap shot photography' which would serve more as a record of your trip versus supporting your adventure promotions in print or online.

If you plan to sell your adventure images, then naturally you'll be looking for the best DSLR you can afford. Most of the top rated DSLRs now shoot 1080 and or 4K video. The choice of extra lenses is yours. Wide angle to zoom.

I tend to go with the iPhone and a small but powerful Lumix point and shoot. I leave the big heavy-duty cameras for road trips. The weight of the camera plus all the lenses and additional kit is just one of those things to factor in when you are on an assignment. If one camera can do it all and do it well, then that is probably the one you take with you. The semi-pro camera will be an excellent investment should you be thinking of selling your images online, from your own website or through a stock photo agency website.

FOCOS App
Just found this app. It is for phones with twin lenses and works especially well for portraits. You can even alter the point of focus after you've taken the shot – great for blurring landscape foregrounds.

The Sony QX100 / QX10 Lens for Smartphones

This lens came on the scene in 2013. If you can find one, they attach to your smartphone and synch with your camera apps. You can hold the lens in your hand to shoot around corners, over the heads of the crowd and all the time view the scene on your phone.

Note re Lumix / Panasonic Cameras

There are many models to choose from ranging from DSLRs to smaller, but powerful and feature rich point and shoot cameras. The point I want to make is that some Lumix models feature a 4K format that allows you to click on any part of the image to refocus it at that point. That is amazing technology and something you might find useful.

The other feature worth mentioning is the zoom capabilities. Some up to 600mm. A tripod would be required to reduce any movement.

Notes:

_____

_____

_____

_____

_____

_____

_____

DRONES AND YOUR NEXT ADVENTURE

Perhaps you have a passion for adventure photography, and you'd like to promote your photographic tours in a new way. Travel photography will never go out of print or style, and if you add adventure into the mix, the result could give you the sales edge you need.

The latest development in camera tech is the drone. Imagine filming your adventures from above. Being followed by your camera in the sky and then showcasing your drone footage on your website to attract new clients.

If you are aware of the types of drones that are flying the skies you might be thinking they are large, professional and you'll need a few thousand dollars in your jeans to buy one. That is true for the pro versions. But wait. Check these out:

Zerotech Dobby Mini Selfie Pocket Drone

This one is the size of your phone and will fit in your pocket. It is the Zerotech Dobby Mini Selfie Pocket Drone with 13MP High Definition Camera U.S. Version with Official Warranty. Price $195

Parrot Disco FPV

What if you could buy a small professional drone for under $700? You simply toss it in the air and off it goes. The Parrot Disco FPV is an easy to fly fixed-wing drone with up to 45 minutes of flight time. It has a 50-mph top speed and FPV goggles. Price $699

USING YOUR ADVENTURE PHOTOGRAPHS TO SELL EVEN MORE TRAVEL

Let's assume you have thousands of adventure images and video clips filed away and perhaps you also have drone footage filed away, too. What to do with it all? How can your turn your photography into new travel sales and also a new source of income? Let's explore.

Generic Advertising and Promotion

When you use your images and video content versus buying it from a stock agency, your credibility goes up. You should always mention the fact that you took the photographs/video so that the reader understands you were there, at the place you are promoting.

The low-to-no-cost use of your photography would be to post those awesome images on social media, create an Animoto video, publish a digital magazine on Joomag and Issue and go big by hosting cinematic events at a local theatre.

Keep the focus on yourself and your adventures and what you want to promote and sell to your clients. When you are actively travelling, photographing, writing and posting your articles, your clients will, in many cases, be pre-sold. Just waiting for your tell-all presentation. It's at that presentation, be it in your agency, at the local hotel, library or theater where you close the sale. Online, you can present using Facebook to run a live show.

Wherever you host your adventure travelogue always factor in a Buy Now component. Ask your preferred suppliers to join you in this promotion.

Building Recognition Through Publishing

Another way to build sales is to publish your photography and your articles and build recognition as an adventure loving writer. You can self-publish so easily today. The hard part is staying focused long enough to complete the articles, the magazine, the book and the DVD.

Once an adventure travel prospect reads about you, gets a glimpse of the trips you arrange and participate in, they will make the call for more information when they are ready to do so.

Once you have published something, email is perhaps the easiest and fastest way to notify your clients/readership where to go on your website to download the files. As you build and grow in the number of publications offer a link to past articles. Archived articles, images and video footage can help sell a present-day adventure.

Becoming Known as an Adventure Travel Writer

It's a different angle, I know, but it can work. The more you become known for your writing about your adventures, supported by your amazing images, the more you will attract a readership. Throughout your articles and magazines, you will promote your next adventure, your custom planning services, and the generic tours your preferred suppliers offer.

Publishing to Amazon and Kindle

Publishing to Amazon, using their CreateSpace self-publishing platform is easy. Very easy in fact. And FREE! The difficult part is writing the book but once you have written it, edited it and it's good to go then you are ready for the next step. You upload it in PDF. You wait two days. You receive an email. You follow the clicks and the next day, your adventure book is selling on Amazon. Now you advise your adventure clients and readership about your new book. Your publication will create new clients, entice existing clients to book another adventure and your book will generate royalties when it sells.

Through CreateSpace you can also publish on Kindle. Photographs and illustrations do not reproduce well on Kindle so you may have to publish just the written word. Think about it though: people are travelling with their Kindle. They want something exciting to read during the flight/ journey and there is your book offering to thrill them.

Note: If you do publish to Kindle you should upload in a file format called EPUB or MOBI. The fastest way to do this is to send your Word document to this company: Word2Kindle.com. Nick Caya is the owner and he will receive your Word document and convert it. Basic conversion cost is $49.

Publishing Your Photography

If people say, "WOW!" when they view your adventure images, then chances are they will sell online. The days of huge money are long gone.

What we have today are the Shutterstock and Storyblocks websites where people and companies go to buy stock photographs and video footage for a small fee. The adventure genre is always in need of exciting and new images. You will not earn huge amounts, however when you investigate successful sellers, they are earning $40,000 a year. The majority would be much lower.

Case in point, I purchased three images for the covers of my three novels and the total cost was USD$49. That price gave me the rights to reprint and use, not own. The images could be sold by the photographer time and time again and through as many stock photo agencies as he or she wanted to list with. All of this applies to you and your images and video footage.

Notes:

BLOGGING FOR ADVENTURE DOLLARS

If you already write an adventure blog then you will know the challenges of maintaining it and keeping the content fresh and exciting. If this is your first blog then you have a couple of decisions to make ranging from how often you will post to your blog, the level of commitment you will need, and the type of content you'll use to attract more adventure readers.

Daily: Be prepared to invest 2-hours each day, minimum.

Weekly: A good choice if you are still selling adventures across the desk.

As and when: You'll post to your blog ONLY when you have something of interest to report, such as just after you led an adventure tour.

Your commitment level: Most blogs die within a few months through lack of commitment and readership.

Keeping it fresh: Plan on-going research for excellent content.

Ideas for engaging the reader: Weave in video and podcasts.

There are thousands of travel blogging sites, and travel blog directories for you to visit and explore. You will quickly find out, as you explore these lists that many blogs are defunct, gone, off the screen and no longer being posted to. The biggest challenge to writing a travel blog is maintaining it, keeping it fresh and interesting and still do your day job – selling adventure travel.

It may suit you better to submit your articles to an existing travel blog. That way you are not having to maintain the blog site or investing quality selling time to promote your blog. If this sounds like a good thing to do then your next move is to locate adventure and generic travel blogs you can write for. Look for directories like the one on the Travel and Tourism Guide website. They list 116 travel blogs and you could add yours. Here's the Travel and Tourism Guide link.

http://travelandtourismguide.com/travel-blog-directory/

TravelPod

Here's a site you might be looking for. Only you will know if it has what you need and want. Give it a click and check it out. www.travelpod.com

TravelBlog

Similar to TravelPod, www.TravelBlog.org offers you a place to create your new blog and typically these websites offer training, workshops, and articles on how you can be a better travel blogger.

Starting Your Own Blog

Last but not least, why not start your own adventure blog from scratch, using a blogging program such as Blogger. It is owned by Google, so your Google account gets you in the door. Once you enter your Google information you will be zapped over to the Blogger set up page. Click on settings, follow all the clicks and within the hour, you should have your own blog up and running. Visit: www.blogger.com

Check Your Website

Have you checked to see if your website host offers a blogging page? They might. I use Weebly for my Selling Travel website and they offer a blogging page. You can post your articles, upload images and insert video. You can also tag it and keyword it and add RSS.

Blogging Books

At the risk of repeating the comment, it's easy to start a blog and very tough to keep it going on a full-time basis AND continue to sell travel.

However, if you start off on the right foot and follow in the footsteps of successful travel bloggers chances are that blogging and vlogging could turn out to be your best form of promotion to sell more adventures.

There are so many books on how to blog that I'd best let you explore online and find the ones that appeal to you. If in doubt, you can always head for the Dummies section. That's right, you can always bank on the For Dummies series to produce a book on the topic and here it is. As always, the Dummies books are thorough. All you'll need to do is factor in the topic of adventure travel.

Notes:

_____
_____
_____
_____
_____
_____
_____
_____
_____
_____
_____
_____
_____
_____
_____
_____
_____
_____
_____

PRESS RELEASES – YOUR SECRET WEAPON

The Press Release is one of my favourite topics in my sales and marketing workshops. The press release should be one of your main marketing tools however, the argument I hear is that there is no way of knowing if your release will be published.

Let's Take Stock

You have done well. Your adventure travel niche is good to go. You have experienced one or two of the adventure products you sell. You have created an adventure blog. You have written adventure travel articles and published your adventure eBook. You have taken amazing photographs and shot excellent video footage. Now you are promoting yourself, your agency, your adventure niche and leading clients and readers back to your website where they can find everything you talk about. Now you wish to widen your scope of influence. Press releases can do this.

Press Release Services

There was a time (and it's still with us) when your press release was subject to the newspaper or magazine editor's decision as to whether or not it should be published. Travel trade veterans will know this; however, times have changed.

Today, just like self-publishing, you can publish your own press releases, anytime. There is no one to stop you from delivering your own press or media release when you submit it to one of the new press release services who will review and edit your press release and then send it. All for a small fee.

These services are tied into mainstream media and social networks. It will work well for you. You should still try the "old way" of sending your press release to local and national newspapers and magazines. You never know. They may like it and publish it.

The PR Web

Basic package starts at $99 per press release. They have editors to review your release and help you get it right. www.prweb.com. Review their How To Write a Press Release articles and let their editors help you when you need advice.

The PR Log

Basic account is FREE and comes with some advertising. You can also embed a video in your release and that's cool and that's FREE too! www.prlog.com

All social media channels are an outlet for your press release. You can post your release, you can link to it and if you wish, record your release on camera and publish a video-release. Check out your favourite social media channels and how they can deliver your press release.

TravPR

The following information comes from the TravPR website: "TravPR.com is pleased to offer a premium online press release distribution service for travel and leisure related businesses at a fraction of the price of the larger online PR  services." TravPR is terrific value. For $34.95 USD you can have your press release zapped around the travel universe and then some: www.travpr.com. Keep in mind, your press release is going out to the travel trade and travel media. This might be where you pitch your adventure images, video footage, adventure travel writing and how-to advice.

Do not hesitate to publish a press release. Yes, it must read right, be spell checked, edited and reviewed before being released. Once that is done, you click, you send and you carry on selling travel. Your press release will surface and it will advise the recipient how they can find you, read you, follow you and best of all BUY ADVENTURE TRAVEL FROM YOU!

PUBLISHING AN ADVENTURE MAGAZINE / TRAVEL FICTION SELF-PUBLISHING WITH ISSUU & JOOMAG

Here is a wonderful self-publishing opportunity that combines your adventure travel writing and your adventure photography. Imagine publishing a digital magazine FULL of your own creative writing.

Your articles should be saved in PDF format, ready for uploading. Click the upload button and wait a few minutes and there before your very eyes will be your flip page digital e-magazine. How nice is that? You are now a digital magazine publisher. Okay, there are few steps between upload and publish, but truly, it is easy to do.

Once the magazine is uploaded to either Issuu or Joomag you can retrieve a code to embed the magazine into your website. You will also find a Share button where additional links can be copied and applied to direct posts to Facebook and more. The overall opportunities are endless.

Here's my Selling Travel page on Issuu. This is just how your magazine account page would look.

Here's what your magazine would look like full screen. The reader clicks the page to turn it, just like reading travel trade magazines online. The Joomag site and layout is very similar to Issuu.

Selling Your Magazine

Both Issuu and Joomag offer an e-commerce opportunity. That means you price your magazine for sale. When readers want a physical copy, they can buy it in soft cover. It is not cheap. The reader would pay about $25 for the magazine and postage. Still, it's something to think about.

Video Pages in Joomag

A reminder, the Joomag platform is slightly different to Issuu in that you can embed videos and audio and flash into the digital page. Imagine your reader turning the e-page to find a video of you hiking along a quiet river embankment in France. All they do now is click on the icon and your video plays for them within the magazine. Pure magic! Your reader does not have to sift and sort online – your video is right there. You can talk to your readers right off the page. Your Joomag issue can also be printed and it's printed by the same people who print for Issuu. Same costs too.

There is another benefit to publishing an e-magazine and that is, once you build the readership to several thousand readers you can approach your preferred suppliers and ask them to advertise with you.

Writing and Selling Travel Fiction

Stay with me now. We're still focused on generating more adventure travel commissions as the main by-product of your photography, video footage and writing skills. We've taken a look at blogging, and publishing press releases and publishing your own eBook and e-Magazines. Now, if you truly have a book in you, how about using your adventure travel background as a theme for a novel. *Travel fiction* as the website below states.

Remember those nights in....? And that wonderful moonlit stroll when you... and.... you know... when you shared your life history... and then one thing led to another... and... HOLD IT! Too much information. You can take it from there. Check this opportunity out – see the link below.

http://www.travel-writers-exchange.com

Imagine if this came true. Now you are an adventure travel fiction or a travel romance writer and how good does that sound? Selling adventure travel, writing novels and building a reader base from your blogs, to your eBooks to your paperbacks and now you are selling upscale adventures. WOW!

Just to show that it can be done, here's my first novel written against the backdrop of my passion, 17th century Japan. The genre is action-adventure. Story line: samurai/ninja vendetta. As the saying goes: If I can do it, so can you.

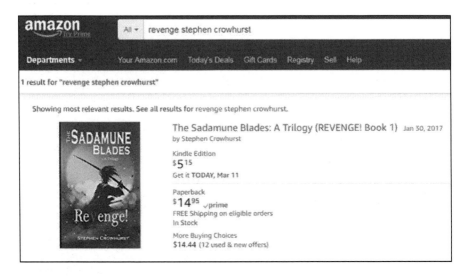

Explore as many adventure guides and novels as you can. Get an idea of what is selling. Check the cover for ideas, too.

Now, back to YOU selling more adventure travel. Once your novel is written, or your guide book for that matter, you can start to use your author status to promote your agency and to attract more clients.

Notes:

YOUR ADVENTURE WINDOW DISPLAY

This can work if you own the agency. If not then you'll be negotiating with your agency owner, manager or head office. The idea here is to use the agency window to promote your travel photography and use the imagery as a call to action. You'll be targeting those consumers driving and walking by your store window.

Imagine this is your agency window. That is your photograph framed and hung in the window. It looks wonderful, consumers are thinking, "I want to go there…" they walk into the agency and start asking questions. I know this works because I used to have my own photographs enlarged and framed on my agency walls.

If your photography is used in this way, the entire agency team can benefit. If you want to focus sell this destination and it's one of your tours that you want to sell, then all the inquiries would come to you.

As you engage the consumer across your desk, you hand them a copy of your latest adventure travel book, your business card, (which has a link to your blog on it) you mention your website and point out where your articles can be found. You now have another reader and hopefully they will refer their adventure loving friends.

Now, everything you've done in terms of setting up shop, travelling, writing, taking photographs and blogging etc., start to converge.

CREATING VIRAL ADVENTURE SOCIAL MEDIA BUZZ

It's not required that you become a social media guru, however it is in your best interest to gain a basic understanding of how social media can help improve your readership and your sales.

A couple of things happen when you put your life on the social line. You will most certainly attract new adventure clients and you will also attract those that like to leave nasty comments. Whether you upload a video, or an article, wherever there is a place to leave a comment – someone will. If you are the type of person who takes such things personally, then you may be better off restricting access to your social media. Only your adventure clients can access your posts. If you wish, you can also disable the comment box.

"You've got to be in it, to win it!" This is the slogan that reminds you that social media **demands** your attention every day. I write about Facebook and YouTube being the two main social media platforms for promoting travel and that is based on the numbers involved and the generations behind the numbers. That said, don't rule out Instagram, Vine, or Pinterest and the rest of the new and trending social media tools. Each has something to offer. The deciding factor is whether or not the end user is adventure minded and has the means to book with you. Here's where I would BOOST what I post to my Author Page on Facebook.

The Social Media Dashboard

With so many social activities and messages to track you'll need help. If you intend to engage all social media then it may prove beneficial to open an account with a service such as Hootsuite. Using a service like Hootsuite allows you to manage all of your social media activities from one source. http://hootsuite.com/

There more than a few competitors to Hootsuite, so over to you to check them out online and decide which one works for you.

Get behind Facebook and study it. It still resonates with your Baby Boomers and even 57% of Gen-Z feel FB has a place in their social life. Click here for more:

http://genhq.com/igen -genz-social-media- trends-infographic/

INVOLVE YOUR ADVENTURE CLIENTS

There may come a time when you need to expand your collection of images and articles. Look no further than your existing and past clients especially if you start publishing your own adventure e-magazine. If you manage a travel agency, you could also involve your agency team.

If you can determine who, out of your client list is a writer, then you could approach them and ask if they would like to contribute to your publication. Most of the time they would write for free and be satisfied just seeing their name in print. Quite often this is all they need as motivation. It also offers boasting benefits when they connect online with their friends. A client's recommendation also sells more travel.

With a stable of adventure clients writing about their adventures a new opportunity presents itself. Why not create an adventure travel writers tour? You have the clients, they have the desire – it's a match made in adventure heaven. Ask your writers where they would like to go. Arrange it and send them off. Better if you join them, then you have more to write about, too.

Now you have fresh content pouring in. The best part is this: your other clients will be inspired by these first-hand accounts as they read about another client sitting with gorillas in the mist, sailing into forgotten island coves, climbing mountains and hiking long lost trails.

As each member of the agency team travel they should make notes for an article to be written when they return. If they can write and travel at the same time, they could email their latest thoughts and comments on and about where they are at that moment in time. Now that would be really fresh content and that is precisely what your clients want.

If the signs are encouraging, why not hire in a well-known author to accompany the tour group. At each stop, hold a workshop. Publish the group's articles in a special issue of your magazine.

A few things are happening here: you have generated new revenues from this trip, you have acquired a writing team, chances are the group will want to travel to another area of the world to write about it and you have a source of excellent content for your magazine PLUS what you write. That's not a bad day's work!

Literary Traveller

If you would like to sell into readymade tours, explore this website. Click to the Literary Traveller. You may be able to sell into their tours and take your travel writing group with you.

http://www.literarytraveler.com/

Notes:

IMAGES TO SCREENSAVERS

Screensaver software gives you the opportunity to turn your adventure photographs and videos into screen savers that sell. Send them out to your clients, readership and social media followers. Annotate your images so your name is always up front. Your screensavers would be appearing on prime-time PC, right about here...

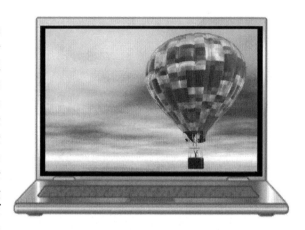

Screensavers can be static and visually stunning. You can add video, QR codes, links and more so that the client looking at your screensaver on their computer screen has instant contact to your articles, website, blog and any other side of yourself you want to promote.

Most screensaver software programs will instantly load your screensaver to the client's desktop once downloaded. If you want to see this in action, you can download a screensaver from one of your preferred suppliers. Yes, your supplier's have been using screensaver technology to spread their brand for many years now.

Think how you can create and update those screensavers each time you travel and write a new post to your blog. You can also promote  your new screensavers via Facebook and Twitter and in your regular client e-mails too. Here's one screensaver program for you to review. One-time cost is USD $39.95.

https://www.blumentals.net/scrfactory/

TRAVEL INSURANCE COVERAGE FOR ADVENTURE TRAVELLERS

TRAVEL SAFETY 101

WHAT EVERY TRAVEL AGENT SHOULD KNOW
ABOUT KEEPING THEIR CLIENTS SAFE

Look for my travel safety eGuide at
www.thetravelinstitute.com

ADVENTURE TRAVEL INSURANCE

This is a product you must know about. Slips, trips and falls have been mentioned as one of the main causes of accidents on the trail. More extreme adventures carry a higher risk and more devastating consequences.

To my mind, and throughout my travel selling career, I have always thought that a travel agent who does not discuss insurance with their client, to be negligent. It is imperative that you, as a seller of adventure travel, become confident in suggesting, quoting, and selling all your adventure clients the best adventure coverage based on the trip they are going to experience. No advice + accident = litigation!

Better your clients invest $100-$300 or more for their personal safety (and hopefully never have to submit a claim) than falling, breaking a leg, and having to pay out of their own pocket to be airlifted out or paying hospital fees and a one-way ticket home.

Your knowledge about adventure travel insurance coverage could also be a niche for you. Some agents in your area will not know too much about it. You could attract their clients to your agency based simply on your knowledge and promotion of adventure travel insurance. It is also worthwhile checking in with your adventure suppliers to review the level of insurance coverage they offer.

I would suggest, when you promote yourself as the local adventure travel agent, that you state up front, in print, on your website and in your social media that none of your clients leave home without adventure coverage. Make a name for yourself using this type of self-promotion. Factor adventure travel insurance into all your promotions.

The following information comes from Damian Tysdal of Travel Insurance Review who has very kindly given me permission to reprint these tips from his website.

http://www.travelinsurancereview.net/trips/adventure/

Adventure Travel Insurance

Travellers who take adventure trips are a whole different breed of traveller. Adventure travel is typically physically demanding and often fraught with personal danger, rustic accommodations, and unfamiliar foods consumed in remote locations. Adventure travel insurance plans are those that include coverage for adventurous activities like hang gliding, diving, skiing, and mountaineering (to name just a few), so it's important for adventure travel tourists to purchase a plan that includes coverage for their planned activities.

What Coverage Does an Adventure Traveller Need?

While the following is not an exhaustive list of all the coverages available with travel insurance plans, it describes those that are most useful to adventure travelers.

- **Evacuation and repatriation coverage** provides the coordination and funds necessary to arrange for a medically necessary evacuation or to return your body home for burial.

- **Medical coverage** provides advance payments or reimbursement for medical and dental care received on your trip – even in a foreign country.

- **Financial default coverage** provides reimbursement for your pre-paid nonrefundable trip costs when a travel supplier ceases operations.

- **Trip cancellation coverage** provides reimbursement of your pre-paid nonrefundable trip costs when the trip has to be cancelled for a covered reason.

- **AD&D coverage** provides a lump sum payment to you or to your family if you are disabled or die on your adventure trip.

- **Travel delay coverage** provides a per-day amount for unexpected lodging, meals and transportation when your travel is delayed a certain number of hours for a covered reason.

What Are the Risks of Adventure Travel?

Some of the unexpected things that can go wrong on an adventure tour include the following:

- **On a trek to Everest's base camp, you experience severe altitude sickness and have to be airlifted off the mountain** – emergency medical evacuations, especially those in remote locations, are highly expensive affairs. Will you have the travel insurance coverage you need or have to pay for it yourself?

- **On a kayak adventure in Costa Rica, you encounter a parasite and become extremely ill** – even if qualified medical facilities are close by, you'll still have to pay for your medical care. Will you have the funds or credit available to cover your medical bills?

- **You pre-paid for a safari but when you arrive, the business is closed** – if the travel supplier you have paid closes up shop and defaults, can you afford to lose that money?

- **You've long planned a SCUBA trip in the Cayman Islands, but the week before you are schedule to leave, a hurricane wipes out your destination** – when a natural disaster strikes, having trip cancellation coverage can ensure you'll receive a refund of your pre-paid trip costs so you can reschedule your trip for another time.

- **You check your bags – including your bike – with the airline, but your bags are stolen before you arrive at baggage claim** – when your clothing, personal items, and sporting equipment are lost, stolen, or destroyed, can you afford to purchase everything you will need to continue your trip?

- **While heli-skiing in Canada, you miss an important turn and are physically disabled** – severe injuries can happen to even the most experienced athletes, and if you are injured to the point of disability, will you have the coverage you need to pay your bills back home?

- **You're on your way to a hiking trip in New Zealand when severe weather causes a temporary shutdown of all flights** – when you've already paid for your trip, having to shell out additional (and unexpected) funds can put a crimp in your travel budget.

ACCIDENTS DO HAPPEN!

That's why we always recommend that you download emergency SOS apps to your smartphone and carry adventure travel insurance in your pocket. Invest in your personal safety today! Contact us for a quote.

There's a start. You can add your creativity to the idea and embellish as you desire. Remember to keep the core message which is to ***invest in your personal safety***. Another reason for selling insurance and trying to keep your adventure clients safe is the commission that insurance pays.

THREE DIE... Just as I was finishing the previous page there was a report of three young Canadians, known for showcasing their adventures on YouTube, have just perished climbing Shannon Falls, British Columbia.

...when a young woman was trying to swim and she slipped and fell. Her boyfriend and another friend went in after her.

It sounds a bit macabre however when you do see these reports in the news and in your social media be sure to collect them and file them away. When you are faced with young adventurers who may believe they are indestructible and beyond travel insurance you can show them that accidents do happen and they happen to experienced adventurers.

These clippings also serve to remind your younger adventurers that going out of bounds, or going too close to the edge can and will result in someone's death. I guess it has to be made clear that regardless of age, bodies don't bounce too well.

Study your adventure travel insurance coverages, meet with your providers and take the training offered.

YOUR JOB NOW IS TO EXTRACT THE INFORMATION YOU NEED AND START WRITING YOUR BUSINESS PLAN AND YOUR MARKETING PLAN.

THE ADVENTURE OF A THOUSAND MILES STARTS WITH ONE STEP CALLED PLANNING

WRITE YOUR THINGS-TO-DO HERE

What are your next steps to get you started on an ADVENTURE SELLING journey? What do you have to do personally and professionally to start on this journey? What is the start date? Complete date? Deadlines? Who is involved?

A good plan is like a road map: it shows
the final destination and usually marks
the best way to get there.

H. Stanley Judd

REFERENCE LINKS
Reference links listed in the order they appear in this book:

Please note, as with all links, websites come and go. If the link is not live when you click there, search for similar names, companies or services.

https://www.adventuretravel.biz/membership/travel-leaders/
http://www.travelmarketreport.com/articles/Survey-Shows-Adventure-Travels-Big-Potential-for-Agents
https://www.adventuretravel.biz/research/2018-adventure-travel-trends-snapshot
www.adventuretravelnews.com/
https://www.intrepidtravel.com/travel-trends-2018/
https://www.globalwellnesssummit.com/2018-global-wellness-trends/
https://cruising.org/docs/default-source/research/clia-2018-state-of-the-industry.pdf?sfvrsn=2
https://www.trekksoft.com/en/blog/9-travel-trends-that-will-drive-the-tourism-industry-in-2018
http://www.travelmarketreport.com/articles/Top-Ten-Destinations-for-Adventure-Travel-in-2018
https://www.technavio.com/
https://www.prnewswire.com/news-releases/global-adventure-tourism-market-expected-to-reach-1335738-million-by-2023-allied-market-research-672335923.html
https://en.wikipedia.org/wiki/List_of_female_explorers_and_travelers
https://www.besthospitalitydegrees.com/30-most-amazing-women-adventurers-alive-today/
https://www.allposters.ca/-sp/The-Conquest-of-Everest-1953-posters_i13184272_.htm
https://www.cineplex.com/CorporateSales/CorporateEvents
https://www.tripadvisor.com/travelmaphome
http://www.travelblog.org/
http://www.worldnomads.com
http://www.adventurefinder.com/adventure-travel/adventure-activities.html
https://greatbritishpublictoiletmap.rca.ac.uk/
https://go-girl.com/
http://www.nationalgeographicexpeditions.com/about/contact
http://www.executiveclasstravelers.com/1/adventure_travel.htm
http://www.specialneedsatsea.com/agents/sng-cata-certification/
http://www.accessibletourism.org/?i=enat.en.news.1910#commentArea
http://www.kantoadventures.com/
https://www.stridetravel.com/hiking-walking-tour-companies
https://localadventurer.com/25-best-hikes-in-the-world-bucket-list/
https://www.wanderlust.co.uk/content/the-worlds-best-walking-routes/
https://www.adventuretravelnews.com/marketing-and-selling-adventure-travel-to-millennials
https://hetravel.com.
https://www.iglta.org/outdoor-adventures/
http://www.alysonadventures.com/about.htm

https://www.intrepidtravel.com/ca/theme/family/single-parent
https://www.us-passport-service-guide.com/minor-travel-consent-form.html
https://travel.saga.co.uk/cruises/ocean/find-your-cruise/solo-travel.aspx
https://www.montanawomensflyfishingschool.com/
https://wildwomenexpeditions.com/
http://www.travelandleisure.com/trip-ideas/adventure-travel/travel-companies-for-women
https://www.rei.com/adventures/trips/womens-trips
https://www.nationalgeographic.com/adventure/lists/9-worlds-most-extreme-adventures/
http://www.touchthearctictours.com
www.webgraphicscreator.com
https://www.mtrip.com/en/tour-operators-travel-agencies/
https://en.wikipedia.org/wiki/Bill_Mason
https://www.climbing.com/people/8-climbing-artists-you-should-know/
www.natgeoexpeditions.com
www.nationalgeographic.com/expeditions/interests/photography/
http://www.nomadphotoexpeditions.com
https://www.exodustravels.com/ca/agents
https://www.outdoorjournal.com/focus-2/insights-female-adventure-photographers-part-1/.
https://www.adventuresmithexplorations.com/small-ship-cruise-travel-agents
http://www.becomeaneventplanner.org/index.html
https://www.worldfoodtravel.org
https://www.epitourean.com/ccts/sign-up
https://www.savoredjourneys.com
www.sellingtravel.net
http://naturetravelnetwork.com/birding-nature-tours/tour-company-classifieds/
http://www.wildbirds.com/Find-Birds/Bird-Tour-Companies
https://www.americanbirdingexpo.com/the-birders-directory-travel-issue-released/
https://wingsbirds.com/
http://www.10000birds.com/
www.ancestry.com
https://www.gozerog.com/
https://www.popsci.com/how-to-become-a-space-tourist#page-5
https://glampinghub.com/types-of-glamping/
http://thetradeshowcoach.com/
www.joby.com
https://www.adventure.travel/film-contest/apply
https://conversationprism.com/
https://en.wikipedia.org/wiki/List_of_social_networking_websites
www.dafont.com
www.1001fonts.com
www.marbleziptours.com/packages
https://www.laughingbirdsoftware.com/
https://issuu.com/smptrainingco/docs/art_of_the_font_a_special
https://www.qr-code-generator.com/
https://mailchimp.com/pricing/

https://www.top10emailmarketingservices.com/
https://mailchimp.com/help/create-a-new-list-group/
https://www.thinkdigital.travel/opinion/gen-z-the-new-destination-disruptors/
https://www.surveymonkey.com/user/sign-up/?fefla=survale
http://www.constantcontact.com/online-surveys/features/create
https://theplanetd.com/youtube-travel-channel/
www.joby.com/store
http://www.iphoneographycentral.com/
https://iphonephotographyschool.com/iphoneography-websites/
www.animoto.com
http://bit.ly/2p5djlm
https://vimeo.com/terms
https://www.youtube.com/static?gl=CA&template=terms
https://www.wikihow.com/Add-a-PDF-to-a-Kindle
www.Word2Kindle.com
http://travelandtourismguide.com/travel-blog-directory/
www.travelpod.com
www.TravelBlog.org
www.blogger.com
www.nuance.com
https://www.ebooks.com/information/authors.asp
https://kdp.amazon.com/self-publishing/help
http://ecoversoftwarepro.com
https://boxshot.com/
www.prweb.com
www.prlog.com
www.travpr.com
www.issuu.com
www.joomag.com
http://www.travel-writers-exchange.com
http://hootsuite.com/
http://www.literarytraveler.com/
www.fineartamerica.com
https://www.blumentals.net/scrfactory/

http://www.travelinsurancereview.net/trips/adventure/
https://www.adventuretravel.biz/?page_id=20663

Champions keep playing until they get it right.
Billie Jean King

About the Author

After a successful career as a travel agent and agency manager with Thomas Cook, agency owner, Director, Business Development & Regional Vice President of Uniglobe Western Canada, travel trade management consultant and trainer with SMP Training Co., contributor to CT Magazine, publisher, artist, photographer, and author, a humourous, no-fluff no-theory keynote speaker edu-entertaining audiences across North America, the UK, Egypt, Bosnia, China, Spain – Steve now focuses on writing travel trade How-To books available through The Travel Institute, and online from Amazon.com. He has been writing how to sell travel articles since 1987.

An adventurer at heart, Steve was outdoors as a kid, then as a teenager he joined his school's outward-bound program led by teacher, Brian Spencer. From those outdoor experiences he learned to hike, climb, kayak and drink cider in a country pub after a day's hike! In 1967 he joined the British Merchant Navy and sailed the world on P&O ships, scrubbing decks, waiting on tables and supervising the swimming pool as the life guard.

In 2017 he published his first novel, Revenge! Book One of The Sadamune Blades Trilogy. In 2018 he published his second novel, Blood Negotiator.

Here are the links to Steve's websites promoting his travel trade how-to eBooks, his novels and his photography. Please visit his websites when you have time.

www.sellingtravel.net
www.stevecrowhurst.com
www.phartography.weebly.com

Other publications by Stephen Crowhurst
Available from www.thetravelinstitute.com

A Travel Agent's Guide to Ancestry Tours
A Travel Agent's Guide to Attracting & Retaining Corporate Clients
A Travel Agent's Guide to Building an Adventure Travel Niche
A Travel Agent's Guide to Prospecting for New Clients
A Travel Agent's Guide to Weddings & Honeymoons
A Travel Agent's Introduction to Attraction Marketing
A Travel Agent's Introduction to Selling Group Travel
A Travel Agent's Introduction to Women Only Travel
FIT and Group Travel Course Bundle
Handy Clip Art and Graphics That Sell Travel
How to Sell More Books with Do-It-Yourself Marketing
PowerPoint Tips for Travel Trade Professionals
Presentation Skills for Travel Trade Professionals
Selling Faith Based, Spiritual & Personal Journeys
Selling Flexible Independent Travel Arrangements
The Travel Agent's Guide to Charging Fees
The Travel Professional's GO VIDEO! Handbook
The Travel Professional's Guide to Managing Your Career
The Travel Professional's Guide to Selling Travel with Humor
Travel Safety 101 – Expecting the Unexpected
Travel Writing for Travel Agents
Using Photography to Sell More Travel
Webinar Presentation Skills for Travel Trade Professionals

THE POWER OF HOW SERIES
How to Close the Sale
How to Publish on Amazon.com
How to Sell Destinations
How to Sell Travel in Uncertain Times

The above titles are digital downloads in PDF format
and can be read on your eReader, tablet and desktop computer.

Travel Writing Travel Agents
is also available in soft cover from Amazon.com.

Since 1964, we've been developing all types of travel industry training for all experience levels – from those new to the industry who need guidance on how to become a travel agent to experienced executives wanting to grow their management and leadership skills. We've earned the reputation as the education destination because our training is relevant, on-demand, and not just the same old stuff.

**The Travel Institute
945 Concord Street
Framingham, MA 01701
Tel: 781-237-0280
800-542-4282
Fax: 781-237-3860
Email: Info@thetravelinstitute.com**

Learn More. Earn More.

https://www.thetravelinstitute.com/